A Traveler's Guide to the Spirit Realm

UNLOCKING THE MYSTERIES TO THE KINGDOM

A Traveler's Guide to the Spirit Realm

UNLOCKING THE MYSTERIES TO THE KINGDOM

MARK VAN DEMAN

DESTINY IMAGE® PUBLISHERS, INC.
P.O. Box 310, Shippensburg, PA 17257-0310

"Speaking to the Purposes of God for this Generation and for the Generations to Come."

This book and all other Destiny Image, Revival Press, Mercy Place, Fresh Bread, Destiny Image Fiction, and Treasure House books are available at Christian bookstores and distributors worldwide.

For a U.S. bookstore nearest you, call 1-800-722-6774.
For more information on foreign distributors, call 717-532-3040.
Or reach us on the Internet: www.destinyimage.com.

ISBN 10: 0-7684-2510-7
ISBN 13: 978-0-7684-2510-9

For Worldwide Distribution, Printed in the U.S.A.

1 2 3 4 5 6 7 8 9 10 11 / 09 08 07

Dedication

This book is dedicated to Jesus. The content is largely His idea. I also want to thank my entire extended family for allowing me the freedom to pursue the Lord as the giver of the Kingdom and the giver of life and truth.

Endorsements

I believe this book is going to be a great help to people who are serious about knowing Jesus Christ in a personal way. To know Him as our Creator and Savior and Lord is our very purpose on this earth and I am truly excited about the way this book explains who He is.

Also, the way in which the path to know Jesus Christ as our Creator is laid out in this book is done in such a way as to make the reader feel as though they are on a grand adventure. And, of course, that is the truth of what those of us who are following Jesus are truly on. I would highly recommend the book *A Traveler's Guide to the Spirit Realm* to anyone who intends to spend eternity with Jesus Christ. It will ignite the excitement in that one to begin the adventure today to know Him, and continue that adventure forever.

Mark Crouch
WCLJ TV42
Trinity Broadcasting Network
Bloomington, Indiana
www.markcrouchministries.com

Mark Van Deman is one of Christendom's best kept secrets. He is supernaturally gifted to not only understand the "deep things of God" but articulate them in a simple, concise, and comprehensive way. Those who read *A Traveler's Guide to the Spirit Realm* and make it applicable to their own lives will be transformed forever.

Bishop J. Laverne Tyson
Senior Pastor, New Beginning Ministries
Indianapolis, Indiana

I read excerpts of this book as it was being written, but upon completion I sat down to read the whole book one morning on a day off. It is a great book to read in a few hours to get the "big picture", but it whets your appetite to delve into further in-depth study of the book. The book opens up another realm of experience and insight for believers of Jesus Christ, inviting them to go deeper—there is much more to know, see, and experience than what they have been exposed to. This is also a great book to draw non-believers into a search for God and a search for truth. It is non-offensive and non-sectarian.

The book was written by a man who began His life-long search for "Truth" at a young age. As a teenager he rejected denominational Christianity because of inconsistencies that he saw. He began to study the Bible to disprove it, but soon discovered that when you truly search for God that you will "find" Him and He will lead you into "all" truth. There is a huge difference between seeking to "know" God and diligently studying the Bible to learn about God, versus merely fitting God into handed-down doctrines or pre-existing ideas about who He is or is not. *A Traveler's Guide to the Spirit Realm* comes out of that life-long search and commitment to "know" God and live for Him in Spirit and in Truth.

Susan Van Deman
(Author's wife)

A Traveler's Guide to the Spirit Realm is an exceptional study guide for new believers as well as those still searching. No matter how secure we may seem in our understanding of life we all struggle with the thoughts of purpose and life after death. Mark has done a great job bringing a mysterious, invisible reality to us in a tangible way. King and Kingdom, concepts we have been made well aware of through media as well as Hollywood, are the foundation of God's empire. Although this is an invisible world we actually can have access to it before we die. What a wonderful enlightenment. This guide will change your life and give true understanding to your journey.

Paul Heimbecker, MD
Into Africa Ministries

I met Mark Van Deman through a precious friend of mine, prophet Russell Winburg—and our acquaintance became quite a journey; a man with nine sons and Susan, his wife, is one of the greatest women I have ever known. Over the next several years and in several nations together, I came to know his character, his dedication to the ministers of his journey, his quest for knowledge and wisdom, and present-tense prophetic vision of the Kingdom.

In my 53 years of evangelism and planting churches, I have seen no greater desire to fulfill the calling of God through Christ Jesus, than a man, like Mark Van Deman, with a vision of His journey in the Kingdom of our Lord Jesus Christ.

Bishop Charles E. Johnson, DD
Founder, Revivals for Jesus Evangelistic Association
Covenant Christian Church Ministries, Inc.
Revivals for Jesus Body Builders International

I believe this book to be a "must read" for all new believers and for those who have not come to know the King and His Kingdom.

This book brought a tear to my eye as I felt the convicting power of the Holy Spirit. His drawing power serves as a witness to me that this is His word to us. I found the pages easy to read and full of enlightenment. Most of all it caused me to hunger to know Him, the King, even more.

I like the way the Study Guide doesn't promote a doctrine, it just invites you to find answers for yourself while offering the thoughts and ideas of the author. I believe this book will cross the boundaries of denominations. I look forward to further studies written by Mark.

Elizabeth Newman
Founder of Zion Ministries

Mark Van Deman gives a very succinct and clear understanding of the key truths related to the Kingdom of God to believers at any level. Uniquely fitted to the national training needs, *A Traveler's Guide to the Spirit Realm* provides an instructional and syllabus format for delivery into the multinational venues encountered by those involved in national training and development. Providing leaders with a much needed resource, the study guide and book will enable people at all levels to gain knowledge of foundational truths found in the scriptures, and then transfer them to the their generation. *A Traveler's Guide to the Spirit Realm* will provide a wide application for its users both here and abroad.

Wade Thompson
Director/President
Living Water Ministries, International

Mark Van Deman is a personal friend and respected colleague who has brought clarity to the mysteries of the Kingdom with the writing of this book. Any Christian, whether new born or mature disciple, would benefit greatly from reading *A Traveler's Guide into the Spirit World*. I would also recommend it as a great resource for group study. My prayer is that each person that is hungry to know Him through greater revelation and wishes to experience the deep treasures of His Kingdom will read this book.

Ralph Douglas
President and founder of Into Africa Ministries

Mark Van Deman offers a spiritually uplifting message in *A Traveler's Guide to the Spirit Realm* as he vividly paints images of what we can expect as the final reward for faithfulness. This message is an inspirational testament with instruction for those seeking to enter a personal relationship with God through Mark's God-given vision. Every chapter appeals to new Christians seeking understanding and long-time believers who frequently drink deeply from the Word. Mark references various scriptural passages emphasizing why God reveals Himself to man so we may know Him and evangelize in His glory. My understanding of God's desire to establish a union with man has been clarified by this book while granting me a new perspective for the significance of Christ's suffering on the cross to bridge the separation between this world and the one beyond mortal comprehension.

John T. Schilawski
High School Assistant Principal
Whiteland, Indiana

Contents

Study Guide Tools for
A Traveler's Guide to the Spirit Realm

Preface

There is no more noble pursuit than the human quest to know the God of all eternity. For the seeker, this quest possesses the mind and soul with such intensity that only a hard run after the truth can satisfy the depths of the longing. Here we find ourselves pursuing that which we must grasp. There is nothing that can keep us from finding Him who surely must be. In our inner man we know that there is more, there must be more. More than meets the eye, more than what we feel, we are certain there is another unseen world where God must be.

This book is written for all those who want to know truth. For those who want to see beyond the here and now, for those who long to know the ever-present One, this text is for you. May the journey into the other realm be richly rewarding. My own experience tells me that nothing else really matters. And so we step forward into the greatest adventure known to man. Let us find Him together.

Your fellow traveler,
Mark Van Deman

CHAPTER 1

The Other World

One of the foundational premises of this book is that another world exists beyond the world we physically live in. This other world is a realm or a sphere that operates with boundaries and laws just like our physical world. Jesus called this world the "Kingdom of God" or the "Kingdom of Heaven." This "Kingdom" will be the destination for our journey. For the adventurous or inquisitive reader, the journey will be a sheer delight.

While some would ask about the differences in these two terms relating to the Kingdom, our purpose is to explore the hidden things of the Kingdom while we experience the dimensions of the hidden world by traveling into it. For my purpose, the Kingdom is the goal we seek. This brings us to the second important facet of the other world we are about to travel in. It has to do with the very nature of the world we will explore.

The realm of our search is not just another world, but it is a Kingdom. And where there is a kingdom, there is a king. Where there is a king, the world operates by His rules and His decree. In this case, our King rules over a world that is not always visible. This Kingdom is eternal and preeminent above all other worlds. The nature of this Kingdom is an expression of the King. Hence, everything within it reflects or embodies who He is.

The existence of this other world as a kingdom has other inherent implications. The fact that this Kingdom of God is ruled by a king tells us something about God. This God is nothing less than a King. He rules authoritatively over His world. He defines the boundaries, the rules, and the life which exists in His Kingdom. For some this might seem elementary. In fact, it is so elementary that most of the world we see has missed it. At the very least, it demands further exploration.

The other world or "Kingdom of God" as Jesus described it is a mystery to most people. While many know that there is "life beyond," they are often uncertain what it looks like. Even those who have strong opinions often have difficulty explaining why they believe as they do. In contrast to the multitude, Jesus described the Kingdom of God on the basis of His firsthand experience. He said that He "came down from Heaven" (John 6:51). What He was saying is that He had come from the world that we are seeking to know about. In my limited experience, I have found that it is always best to get directions from someone who has already been where I would like to go. The life and words of Jesus will become our filter, our amplifier, our telescope, and our inter-preter for this new world experience. As we explore this hidden world, we will find that He holds the keys to the mysteries of this Kingdom.

CHAPTER 2

The Way In

If there is another world, there must be a way in. This simple and logical perspective has always been understood among adventurers, pioneers, explorers and the inquisitive among us. It seems as if there is a yearning deep within us that cries out to know what is beyond. Most of us would love to meet someone who could lead us to the destination or source of truth. If only someone could unlock the door to the other world.

As I have traveled along this path, I have discovered that we need a guide who can take us into the hidden world of the spirit. As we prepare to travel into another culture or another country, we normally rely on someone else to get us in. We rely on a travel agent, an airline pilot, a government official, or somebody "in the know" to help us.

There is no such thing as a person who arrives at their destination alone. If we are going to travel or explore we need someone we can trust to help us get there. I have personally met a guide that is trustworthy and has come from this hidden world of the spirit.

The guide that has taken me into the hidden realm of the Kingdom of God is Jesus. He is a historical person who continues to live mysteriously in ways we will discuss as our journey unfolds. Every adventure and every reality begins with a set of assumptions as a starting point. As a seasoned traveler in the spirit world, I can simply say from personal experience that Jesus lives and is a reliable guide. He will help us as we seek to enter the Kingdom of God. This assumption is scientifically verifiable by my experience as well as the personal experiences of many others throughout the generations who have made this same journey.

The purpose of this discussion is to help us get in. We can't do it alone. We can't understand the other world without a guide, a helper, or a friend. It's because the other world was created by a King who made the rules of dependence, interconnectedness, and relationship. The King has decided that we can't come in without an escort, a ticket, an advocate, and an invitation. Like it or not, there is a protocol to enter the Kingdom. For this reason, many will stay outside and miss the life that exists within the hidden Kingdom. The foolish stubborn pride of some people will rob them of all the beauty and treasure that was available for them inside the hidden Kingdom. This brings us to the entrance into the Kingdom of God.

The way into the hidden realm of the spirit is described in different terms by different people. I personally prefer to describe the entrance requirement as the way of humility. Every person who seeks to enter the Kingdom of God must humble themselves. What this means is simply that no one is allowed in the Kingdom of God unless they ask for help. We begin our journey by simply asking for help and the directions we need to enter this hidden Kingdom of God.

Everyone that enters the Kingdom of God must ask for this assistance to be brought in to the Kingdom. The King provides a personal escort for us. No one is allowed to enter into the Kingdom of God without this personal escort and the ticket that He has personally paid for in full. I will explain this more in detail later, but for now, we need to simply follow the instructions and follow the escort who has obtained our tickets for us. Our ability to follow Him is directly related to our ability to discover the realities we seek. Our guide will also become our advocate and escort who will lead us into all truth.

There is one more curious thing about the Kingdom. An invitation is required from the King in order to enter. No one is allowed in to the Kingdom of God without a personal invitation from the King. He declares that we may come in because of what He did to get us in. No one is allowed in unless they have heard Him personally invite them into His world. Until we receive the invitation, we are not allowed to enter. Somehow, we must hear that invitation or that voice in our inner man so we can come in to the Kingdom. Unless we hear this voice of invitation, we will remain outside.

This is all leads us to one final mystery connected to the protocol of the Kingdom. Although we must first receive an invitation to enter the Kingdom, there is still the issue of our decision that determines our experience. The King has determined that we enter the Kingdom when we want to enter. While He places the "want to" inside of us, he leaves the final decision up to us. In order to enter we must lay aside our rugged independence and cry out for help. It is as if we must say, "I know that I am invited, but let me in please!" Our desire launches us into the place where we are helped into the Kingdom.

We could summarize the whole process by saying that the way into the hidden realm of the spirit is essentially within us. If we are willing to humble ourselves and trust Him as our friend, He will take us in. The decision is given to us. The process involves humility and a willingness to follow. Like every adventure, there is a starting point with a few given assumptions. We enter the Kingdom with a trustworthy guide who will escort us into truth. We are invited by the King but only enter when we want to. The primary question really becomes, do you want to go in?

CHAPTER 3

Through the Door

Houses, cities, and realms have gates or doors through which we enter. We come into almost everything through some type of passageway. The Kingdom of God has its own door, its own special passageway. If we want to enter, we must come through the door which the King has selected as the designated way into this realm of the spirit and into His Kingdom.

This world of the spirit is legally entered only one way. Jesus made a revealing statement when He said "I am the way..." (John 14:6). In typical exclusive language, Jesus declared that He was not just one of the many optional paths, passages, or gates. He declared that He was "the way." We could add the word "only" in so much that other ways lead elsewhere, not to God, not to Heaven, and not to life. While there may be other ways or doors, these lead to destruction or dead ends, while He leads to life. Jesus declared that He would take the seeker into the spiritual world where truth and life could be discovered. Jesus then becomes not only our guide to the other world, but literally the door into it.

Throughout history, men have said that Jesus was a great teacher. They should hear His words when He said, "I am the door, if anyone enters through Me, he will be saved..." (John 10:9). Clearly the Bible teaches us that Jesus was very specific in His thinking. Some people would even say that Jesus was "narrow-minded." The politically correct would strive to be broad and inclusive. Nevertheless, Jesus said, "Strive to enter through the narrow door; for many, I tell you will seek to enter and will not be able" (Luke 13:24). In another setting Jesus said, "Narrow is the gate and difficult is the way which leads to life, and there are few who find it" (Matthew 7:14). The way into the other world is through Jesus, but it is not easy. While it may be difficult in some aspects to enter the Kingdom through Jesus, it promises great rewards. This mystery demands our focus and study.

Perhaps it would be helpful for us to consider the easy and the hard parts of entering into the Kingdom of God. After all, it is totally possible that certain aspects of a thing could be both difficult and yet easy at the same time. For example, most of us could jump into the sea, but not all of us can swim to shore. This dynamic tension is apparently a reality as we prepare to enter the Kingdom of God. The easy part has to do with the one who takes us in. As we discussed in Chapter Two, Jesus is all we need to get in. Jesus is the guide, the advocate, the one who pays the price for our ticket, and the advocate who sticks with us at all times. He is also the way and knows the way. He is the door and has invited us in. All this sounds pretty easy. So what then is the difficult part? The difficulty has to do with the change that must occur in each of us before we can enter.

Jesus said "unless you are converted and become as little children, you will by no means enter the Kingdom of Heaven" (Matt. 18:3). For many people, the idea of conversion is challenging because it requires change. It means changing old, worn out ideas for Kingdom ideas. It means changing loyalties from old gods to the Living King who is called "The One True God." It may mean changing friends to those who are seeking life instead of those who live with deadly habits and self-destructive lifestyles. Conversion requires a complete remaking and renewing of the old man who was trapped in this present world system. A converted person thinks Kingdom, talks Kingdom, and acts Kingdom. We could say that a converted man acts "other worldly." The Kingdom person becomes a brand new person. For many of us, the converted person is much nicer! Having said these things, we can proceed to the second difficult part of the transformation process.

Jesus said that "you must become as little children" to enter the Kingdom of God (see Matt. 18:3). We must understand what children are like in order to understand what Jesus meant by His teaching. Children are usually teachable, willing to be led by another, and totally dependent on their caretaker. Children are often innocent in their ways and accept things without skepticism or doubt. Children tend to accept other children without prejudices that adults have learned. In many ways, children are ready followers. These natural attributes of children tend to diminish in the growing-up process, as we often think in terms of adulthood as being a stage of lost innocence. But now we come to the converted man who is about to regain His innocence. He regains His childhood purity along with becoming teachable through the conversion process. This conversion experience allows a totally renewed being to exist. How does this happen?

For a person to become as a child, he or she must relinquish control of their life to another. A Kingdom man relinquishes control of His life to the King of the Kingdom. The Kingdom woman releases her right to choose to the King who makes right choices for her. The Kingdom person becomes dependent on the King by forming a dynamic relationship with Him. Instead of a stubborn *independence*, there emerges a healthy *interdependence*. The Kingdom person understands that he or she must be taught all over again. He must learn the entire language, culture, and way of life which the King has established for His people. This process requires a willingness to learn new ways of thinking and acting. While becoming "like a child" may be difficult for some people, it is still necessary. This brings us to the final requirement for entering the Kingdom.

Before the child begins to grow he must first be born into this new world. In the very words of Jesus, "...you must be born again" (John 3:7). For some people the most challenging concept of conversion is often described as the "new birth experience." It appears as if the challenge of a "new birth" is often an assault on human pride. It is said that a notable teacher asked Jesus, "How can a man be born when he is old?" (John 3:4). The human ego hates to admit that part of who we are never started to grow. The thought that we might possibly be incomplete is deplorable to the proud and self-sufficient. Nevertheless, we are missing something that can only be added through "rebirth." The missing *something* is a man born totally of the spirit. Only a spirit-born man can enter a Kingdom which is essentially spirit. Thus, the great mystery of entering the Kingdom on the basis of being "born again" becomes foundational in the journey. Simply, one must be born into this other world, this Kingdom of God, in order to have any understanding about it.

When we consider the concept "you must become as children," we understand that conception and birth are initial stages of childhood. A person enters the Kingdom of God through Jesus, the door. We come to Him for help. We receive cleansing from the filth of the world. He clothes us with heavenly attire. He receives us as His own. He enters our life. He produces a new man inside the outward physical man. A spiritual man is conceived and born within us. This new man who is "born from above" is now able to develop into a true child of God. Everything in the Kingdom that he is born into belongs to Him as a citizen of that Kingdom. The child of God is an heir of this new world, even though the child knows very little about it. The difficulty of birth has brought forth new life. I will say from experience, when we see the treasures in the Kingdom it is all worthwhile.

One of the most amazing facts about the Kingdom of God is that every child born into this Kingdom is wealthy. The treasures that are part of the Kingdom of God are reserved primarily for the children who are citizens of the Kingdom. Only on a rare occasion does a visitor catch a glimpse of the hidden riches within the Kingdom. Any glimpse of the Kingdom has only one purpose for the prospective child of God. Each glimpse of the treasures within the Kingdom is designed to be an invitation. When the curtain of the Kingdom of God is pulled back, it is intended that the onlooker will enter the door. Entrance necessitates a new birth experience. The voice of Heaven is speaking to the hearts of men and women: "Come in." There is a treasure within. The guide is waiting. "He will guide you into all the truth" (John 16:13). Now is the day to come into the Kingdom. If you have not already taken the first step, ask Jesus now to make you a brand-new person. If you ask Him to make you a child of God, He will do it. Ask, believe, and it will be done for you. Believe and receive. Now begin to thank Him that it is done! New life has just begun! Now the journey truly begins.

CHAPTER 4

The Treasure Within

For those who have believed, the life of God has birthed us into His Kingdom and into His world. As children of God, we have entered the invisible spirit world. As we enter this other world, we are quickly overwhelmed with the wealth, the beauty, the expanse, and the wonder of it all. Every direction we look, we see infinite treasures like lush beautiful fruit and an indescribable creation. The first day in the Kingdom of God for many new believers is almost surreal. It is almost beyond our wildest dreams. Here we are, still living in a physical body in "the real world" while the new man inside of us is peering into the whole spirit world. Our inner man may feel like a child who is visiting an amusement park for the very first time. Amazement and awe resound inside us.

When our spiritual eyes first open, the world of His Kingdom seems brilliant and breathtaking. Everywhere we look, the King has placed His hand upon His creation. We see fingerprints beneath the surface of this present world while others may not even know that a hidden Kingdom exists. It is almost like having infrared night vision goggles that allow one to see in the dark. Kingdom people see what the people of this present world are unable to see. Vision is one of the first gifts a child of God receives from the King of the Kingdom. As we gaze at the hidden world, our inner man shouts, "How sweet it is!"

About the same time that we begin to see, we suddenly realize that we can also hear. We hear our King and guide who is talking to us directly. We look around to see Him, but all we can hear is His voice. This is initially very strange. We hear Him, but we don't see Him. Then it occurs to us that we are now hearing from within. This is surely different! In the physical world, we are told that people who "hear voices" are crazy. Now we hear His voice clearly. Jesus said, "He calls His own by name and leads them out. And when He puts forth all His own (sheep), He goes before them and the sheep follow Him because they know His voice. And a stranger they simply will not follow..." (John 10:3-5 NASB).

The imagery of a shepherd with His sheep is used to describe a marvelous reality in the Kingdom of God. The guide who is leading us is also the Good Shepherd. He assumes all the caregiver activities and responsibilities of a shepherd to His flock. His voice is the voice of comfort, security, provision, and well-being. In the Kingdom we follow a leader who is totally trustworthy and caring. He knows that we can only follow Him if we first learn to hear His voice. Our ability to hear Him is critical for survival. This is why He gives "ears to hear." As He speaks to us we quickly learn to obey because we know that He is watching out for us. We see that He is totally trustworthy. Time and time again, He speaks to us as His own little children. He leads us to all the places we need to go. He tells us amazing things about His creation as we follow Him closely. As He speaks, everything around us comes to life. The colors get brighter, the path becomes clearer, and the sense of peace intensifies within us as we learn to appreciate this One who cares for us. And when we least expect it, He begins to reveal His plans and purpose for all creation that once seemed so mysterious to us all. It is here where the revelation of plan and purpose converge in the journey that we will soon discover the greatest treasure in His Kingdom: the love of God.

As we travel through this glorious Kingdom we experience something like a vast and marvelous ocean that is pure and clear which extends forever. It is an amazing representation of an endless attribute of the King which seems to flow in every direction. We are experiencing a most unusual and yet recognizable quality of the King and His Kingdom. We have discovered the love of God which is tangible, but almost impossible to fully describe.

This love of God that is so vast and infinite is not only pure, but continually refreshing and full of life. It is like the ocean in that the quality in the shallowest of water is identical to the deepest part of the sea. The first step into His love is as sweet as the next and so on. It is a love that never varies in quality. It only deepens in intensity and volume. There is always more of it to be experienced. It is like unending perfection. There is enough for everyone. It is mysterious in that it is far more than a feeling or sensation. It is tangible and yet intangible. As we observe the reality of the love of God, it is as if people seem to experience it in many different ways. Some people seem to play in it. Some people seem to drink it. Some people bathe in it. People swim in it. People float in it. Others dive deep into it. Some explore it, but none can ever really ignore it. The gift of Kingdom life and love cannot be contained, restrained, or really even explained. It is truly something that is unfathomable. It can only be received and enjoyed and shared with others. Oh the treasure of the riches of the love of God! The Kingdom of Heaven is many things, but surely it is a Kingdom of love.

CHAPTER 5

The Treasure in Him

In the initial days of Kingdom discovery, one of the most marvelous revelations is the depth of the guide who is the King of this Kingdom. As He personally conducts the tour of His world which is becoming our world, we find the subtle reality that His Kingdom is not without, but rather within. To our amazement, it is in us and in Him. The realm of His rule with all the vastness of its treasure resides in Him. To the natural mind this is almost incomprehensible. Not only are the treasures hidden in Him, but He is with us and leading us onward while simultaneously existing within us. Therefore, all that our spiritual eyes behold are seen through Him while looking out and looking in at the same time.

Jesus Himself said to His hearers that "the Kingdom of God is in your midst" (see Luke 17:21). Wherever the King is, the Kingdom of God is present. Secondarily, where the King is, all the treasures of Heaven exist. There is a wealth and richness in Him that abides continually for the child of the Kingdom. Our discoveries in His kingdom will make us truly rich, "attaining to all the riches of the full assurance of understanding, to the knowledge of the mystery of

God, the Father and of Christ in whom are hidden all the treasures of wisdom and knowledge" (Colossians 2:2-3 NKJV).

The exploration of the Kingdom reveals that the guide who is the King is full of wealth, treasure, and wisdom. He is also a Father who gives good gifts to His children. We gladly find ourselves to have been adopted by a great king who delights to lavish His abundance upon His family. (See Ephesians 1:3-9). The wonder of our experience deepens with each marvelous revelation of what we have stepped into. By His own kindness, the King of all Kings has invited us into the realm of His life. It is precisely at this point that a grateful sense of awe envelops us as we begin to experience Him. Our spiritual journey now produces more than excitement, it produces joy.

Perhaps the growing amazement we have is at the privilege of being in His presence. Gratitude begins to overtake us. When we began the journey, it never occurred to most of us how kind this King of Glory was to invite us into His world. We knew there was more than our eyes could see, but few realized that this "other realm" was the home of such a magnificent King. Little did we know that our entrance into this world was a part of His plan to make us part of His family. Not many of us realized that beyond "the door" a wonderful King was waiting to share all the riches of His Kingdom with us. We know that our entrance into His world had nothing to do with our deserving anything. In His kindness, He simply made room for us to be with Him.

Nevertheless, we are now seeing all that we have in Him and in His Kingdom. We also have this sense that half has not yet been told of what awaits us. It finally occurs to us that He is more than just wealth and wisdom and love personified. He is everything we have ever hoped for. He is the fulfillment of our deepest longing.

Eventually it begins to make sense. The vast ocean of love we had first sensed flowing in all directions comes out of Him who is Love. Everything in the Kingdom radiates His loving-kindness. The gifts, fruit, and treasure mirror the Master. His Kingdom is a Kingdom of love and beauty. His Kingdom is a world of perfections. His Kingdom is a place where dreams and hopes come true. This is truly another world! The atmosphere of the Kingdom is an atmosphere of love. Everything within His Kingdom is born of love and sustained by love.

With this marvelous awareness we want to know more. We want to know where all this love came from. We yearn to know how this world came to be. As we study Him who leads us in this Kingdom, we also notice a peculiar thing about the King. While everything in the world seems perfect, His hands and feet bear the scars of nail wounds visible to the human eye. Where did these nail scars come from in such a perfect Kingdom? There is surely an explanation for the mystery of the scars which He wears with humility yet with an aura of triumph like the medals of a war hero.

CHAPTER 6

Colliding Kingdoms

In order for us to understand the hidden Kingdom, we must hear from the King about His scars. The story of the King and His scars is well known to most seasoned spiritual travelers. For our purposes, we can simply say that the mystery is revealed in the oldest book which men call The Bible. This is the essential overview of the story.

When the Creator first made man, as King He gave every man freedom of choice. The Creator's desire was simply to walk with man who was created for friendship. The nature of choice implies a freedom to go one's own way. As man was given this freedom, he sought independence and a life apart from the Creator. Selfish choices eventually led to certain destruction and eventually, death for men who had once been created to know life and the giver of life. With the first wrong choice came a kingdom at war with the Creator's Kingdom. The fallen earthly kingdom was birthed as a natural realm over which man would rule yet death would always be its final result. Men set themselves up on thrones of their making in attempt to control their lives. Men and women who were unwilling to yield to the Creator's plans and purpose became the opponents of the King and His eternal Kingdom. Self became king in man's fallen order, only to discover that life without the Maker is no life at all.

The central storyline in the Bible tells us that the Creator King who was rejected by self-centered men and women still longs for relationship. Even though the two worlds collided, the Creator's unstained perfect love for man never ceased to look for a way of reconciliation. In His infinite wisdom, the King chose to bridge the gap with His own life. He knew that He alone could save the human race from selfishness, death, and self-destruction. As we read His story, we see that He brought about this salvation through His own personal entrance into human history. History is based on His story.

The story of the King's entrance into man's fallen world is truly a great mystery. He chose to enter by wrapping Himself in a vulnerable infant's body to be brought forth through a young virgin in Israel some two thousand years ago. The plan was not some divine afterthought, but purposed from the beginning of time according to the Bible. The child of the virgin was named "Jesus" because it was said that He would save His people from their sins. The miracle of incarnation is that the Creator became one of us, that we as men could become one with Him. This Jesus was born as the Creator in human flesh with a mission that would reconcile fallen man to the Creator King.

As we study the earthly life of Jesus we quickly see the reality and supremacy of His Kingdom over the present world of man. The mysteries of the invisible realm are embodied in the man Jesus who is called "the Word made flesh" (see John 1:14). Those mysteries are revealed by His life, His teaching, His death, and ultimately His resurrection from the dead. As King Jesus invades the fallen order of men, we see Him conquer every foe. Furthermore, we continually see the very nature and character of the Creator King in every facet of His life. In Jesus we see the nature of One who has left His eternal and invisible Kingdom to pursue the ones he loves despite the cost to Him personally. We see perfect love personified as he lays aside His Kingly garments to take on the role of One who serves among the least of men. We are gripped by the unselfish and fearless way Jesus takes the entire responsibility of mankind upon Himself. In an ultimate act of unselfish love, He pours out His own life to bring us back to the Creator and the eternal Kingdom. This marvelous story of reconciliation takes place with a most unusual plot and conclusion as we will soon discover. Only One who lives outside this present realm could have designed such an amazing plan of redemption.

CHAPTER 7

The Cross

The ultimate act of unselfish love was displayed on a Roman device for execution. Two timbers were connected as its rough wooden beams provided the means for ancient Roman justice to be carried out. The main beam was placed in a hole which had been dug to make the Cross a public spectacle for execution and shame. The crossbeam rested across the shoulders of the condemned man near the top of the upright beam. The upright Cross with its perpendicular members symbolically pointed upward to eternity while reaching horizontally to all mankind. On a cross like this, Jesus was crucified and died in the presence of many witnesses. The scars are the reminder that He hung there bleeding and bruised in order to bring about a plan that only Heaven fully understands.

In order to help us understand just a little, we must first see the Cross as a place of justice. Criminals paid for their crimes on this cruel execution device. The Cross was the tool for capitol punishment in Roman times. Many people wonder how the innocent Jesus ended up on the Cross with a sentence of death. Essentially, Jesus paid the price for the sins of the world on the Cross. As we will progressively discover, the only way to really understand this story is to see the entire event as the intersection of divine justice and infinite love.

After three years of teaching and performing great miracles, Jesus had developed a great following of friends as well as opponents. Even though many rejoiced to embrace His Kingdom, others were threatened by his powerful message. As one might expect, greed and jealousy were among the motives that led to the crucifixion of Jesus. Evil men conspired together with false accusations and lies until Jesus was eventually tried and condemned by a Roman ruler. Though he was innocent, Jesus was condemned to die on the Cross.

While the whole story is both horrible and marvelous at the same time, the most remarkable thing in the entire biblical narrative is that this horrible event was part of the Creator's plan from the beginning of time. Jesus even knew in advance that He would suffer and die and spoke of His pending death prior to the event. This mystery can only be grasped if we see the entire event outside of time and space from a Heavenly perspective.

For the Creator to restore fallen man, a satisfaction of divine justice was required. Man by His selfish choice has sinned and separated Himself from the perfect world of the Creator King and His eternal Kingdom. Only a sinless perfect man could restore the broken fellowship between God the Creator and fallen man. The only perfect man capable of intervening was Jesus. He alone was capable of offering Himself as a substitute for the fallen world because he had lived a sinless holy life. We could say that the just died for the unjust on the Cross. Jesus satisfied the legal requirement for sin as "the wages of sin is death" (see Romans 6:23). He paid the ransom price for every man. He tasted death for every man. On the Cross outside Jerusalem on that day, Jesus carried the sin of the world on His own body, "and by His stripes we were healed" (1 Peter 2:28). His back was beaten raw, His hands were nailed to the cross, His beard was plucked out, and He died for us all that day. Beyond the horror of this dreadful scene, the unthinkable was about to take place. Except for the angels and those on the other side, no one could anticipate the great awakening that was about to occur. In three days, all Heaven would break loose!

CHAPTER 8

Up From the Grave

One great mystery of the eternal Kingdom is that the only way to truly live is to die first. Jesus said for a man to save his life, he must first lose it. A similar saying declares that unless a kernel of wheat goes into the ground and dies, it would remain alone. These teachings of Jesus become evidence to us that Jesus knew in advance that His own life would be given as a ransom for those sold into the slavery of sin and death. Jesus knew that he would suffer and die for the sins of the world. He also knew that he would live again as would all those who believe. This is why He said, "I am the resurrection and the life. He who believes in Me, although he may die, he shall live. And whoever lives and believes in Me shall never die" (John 11:25-26).

The King said that He would live and live He did!

On the third day after the crucifixion of Jesus, the grave could no longer contain the One who had made Earth and Heaven. The King of life broke the chains of death as life now surged again through His immortal body. The One who had died was now raised to life. Resurrection power exploded from the tomb of death. Death was conquered as the King of Life triumphed over every enemy including death. The King of Life had invaded the dark world and won. He bridged the great divide to open a door of Heavenly life to all those who would be His friend forever. To all who received Him, "to them He gave the right to become children of God, to those who believe in His name" (John 1:12). Suddenly, true friendship between God and fallen man could take place. The King of creation had become the reconciler of two opposing worlds. He had paid the price to ransom man with His own blood. Now men could legitimately enter the realm of life and live for eternity.

Jesus who had died was now alive forevermore. Resurrection life was now available to every person that desired to become a true friend of God. The door to the "other world" of His eternal Kingdom stood open for all to enter in. He only asked man to believe. He promised abundant and eternal life to everyone that would believe in Him then follow in simple faith. The Creator yearned for a relationship with mankind that would be built on His own unselfish love. In return, men and women would trust Him and follow in confidence and faith. The eternal foundation for man to be reconciled to God was laid at the Cross. The relationship of eternal life with God is built on trust in the One who offers it freely. Life in the Kingdom flows forth from the King. His life is resurrection life that knows no limits. The resurrection is the foundation of all life and truth for those who follow Him. This too is a great mystery, but it is one that has been experienced for generations by countless numbers of those who have entered the Kingdom of God.

CHAPTER 9

The King and the Kingdom

It has become increasingly evident that the mysteries of the Kingdom are internally connected to the mysterious King. The greater our understanding of the King, the more we can live and move in the realm of His Kingdom. The beauty of understanding the Kingdom is that it produces life now. This resurrection life that King Jesus offers every man is not just for some future day, but for today. The Heavenly Kingdom is now made open to every believing man, woman, boy, and girl. King Jesus said, "The Kingdom of Heaven is at hand" (see Matt. 3:2). He was saying that the Kingdom is near enough to reach out and grab hold of it. We can enter the world of King Jesus, partake of His resurrection life, and explore the mysteries of His Kingdom as we get to know Him. In order for us to really experience this life, we must know the King.

We have already seen how the Creator King enters history in human flesh and is called "Jesus." To say it another way, King Jesus is God in flesh. The Bible declares, "The Word (of God) became flesh and lived among us... full of grace and truth" (John 1:14). God in the flesh is a mystery of mysteries. When God becomes incarnate in man His name is called "Jesus." Who else could tell us about God's world better than God Himself? It is no wonder that the primary teaching emphasis of Jesus is upon the Kingdom of God. This was at the heart of His earthly teaching ministry. To verify the validity of His teaching, Jesus usually demonstrated His power with an accompanying miracle. Upon one occasion Jesus actually spoke to a stormy sea and the wind and the waves died down as He spoke. His friends who were seasoned fisherman became fearful as the storm quickly ceased. They then asked one another, "Who is this man that even the wind and the sea obey Him?" (Mark 4:41).

Jesus had begun His three years of earthly ministry by proclaiming the centrality of His Kingdom. (See Mark 1:15.) He uses the terms "Kingdom of God" and "Kingdom of Heaven" as interchangeable ways to describe the hidden realm of the spirit. Even after His resurrection, the important earthly ministry concludes with forty days of teaching "things pertaining to the Kingdom of God" (Acts 1:3). Jesus had earned the right to rule over His eternal Kingdom. His life of perfection and His sacrificial death proved that he was fit to rule as King over all kings. His resurrection validated His claim as ruler or "Lord of all". He was declared the Son of God with power by the resurrection from the dead (see Romans 1:4). He had lived and proved that His Kingdom was not "of this world", yet it is the greatest kingdom ever known to man.

Indeed Jesus fulfilled the prophetic words of Daniel the great prophet and statesman of Israel. These words were written some six hundred years before

Jesus walked the face of the earth, "His Kingdom is one which will not be destroyed" (Daniel 6:26). The supremacy and longevity of His Kingdom is grounded in the reality that Jesus came to earth as God in the flesh. His Kingdom is an everlasting Kingdom. The Kingdom of God awaits those who make friends of the King. No friendship is as important or rewarding as a friendship with the King. No kingdom will ever compare to the Kingdom of God our King.

CHAPTER 10

Friends of the King

The Cross on which King Jesus died makes the ultimate statement of God's desire for friendship with man. Jesus said, "No greater love does a man have than he lay down His life for a friend." He personally demonstrated the greatness of His love for man when He laid down His life on the Cross. The death of Jesus on the Cross not only reconciled two Kingdoms that were truly worlds apart, but made friendship between God and man a possibility. The "God-man," King Jesus, came to teach us the secrets of true friendship.

As we consider all the relationships known to man, it would seem that friendship is the highest order of all possible relationships. From the standpoint of choice, we don't decide who will be our family as a rule, but we can decide who will be our friends. Even in the context of marriage, many couples learn the deep value of friendship together only after many years of being together. Some of the greatest eternal realities are concealed in the bonds of friendship. Perhaps one of the most marvelous mysteries of the Kingdom of God unfolds when we realize that the King wants to be our friend.

The eternal resurrection life that Jesus offered man is ultimately rooted in His desire for friendship. The Creator wanted more than justice and reconciliation. He wanted a dynamic loving relationship. The King desired a life that could be shared. This shared life is at the center of friendship. In the life of two friends, nothing is withheld from the other. A true friendship is built on trust and confidence. In this arena, anything can be openly and honestly discussed. Friendship demands an environment of vulnerability, acceptance, and unconditional love. As a true friend, God gives us a choice to walk with Him. While the Cross is the gateway to friendship with God, man must continually choose to sustain the relationship with devotion and faithfulness.

While the possibility of friendship with God the Creator King is exciting, the implications for man are truly amazing. God wants man to enter His world. He literally invites us to come over to His place. As a true friend He wants to share what He has with us. Of course He wants to "show us around." It is His desire to show us the entirety of all that He has made and everything that He owns. He wants us to feel at home in His Kingdom world. It is His desire to share His innermost thoughts with those who would dare draw near to Him. He wants to tell us His plans and share His dreams for His creation. He wants us to know that if we stay with Him, everything we ever need will be totally provided. This is the place in God where fellowship and friendship truly merge.

On the human side of friendship with God, there is ample room for our devotion to Him to be expressed in simple ways. He initially asks us to trust Him and follow Him. The implication is that we believe that He is in control and will lead us into life. His leading comes from within as He takes residence in our innermost being. Secondarily His leading comes from the Bible. As we follow His simple directions we enter life and begin to know Him in many new ways. We begin to understand that our friendship involves doing the things that we know would please Him. We are also eager to do the things He asks us to do as we begin to clearly recognize the many ways He may communicate with us. A real relationship of yielding and caring develops in the space of time. Ultimately we enter into the depths of friendship for which we were made. This is the goal of God. This is the fullest sense of the meaning of salvation and the purpose for which we are created. It is the very reason that Christ Jesus came into the world.

For those who enjoy Bible study, we recommend a survey of those who were considered to be among the closest to God. In the case of many great Bible characters, we see that "friendship with God" set them apart from others. Abraham was called a friend of God. The Bible tells us that God spoke to Moses as a man speaks to His friend, face to face. When Jesus walked the face of the earth, He was called a friend of sinners. The progression of the biblical narrative shows us that the highest order of friendship is the one we have with Jesus. Those who are friends of Jesus are the ones He entrusts with His message and life. What began as friendship between Jesus and only a few fishermen became a model for friendship with all that would receive Him. God wants us to choose Him today. Perhaps the real question becomes, will you be a friend of God?

CHAPTER 11

Chosen

Sometimes the thought of being a friend to God can be overwhelming. When we consider that any such idea comes from God Himself, the thought is even more amazing. Consider the statement from Psalm 4:3, "The Lord has set apart the godly man for Himself." Friendship with God originates with God's choice. He reveals Himself. He chooses to be made known. He chooses to become the initiator of a relationship with man. It is initially and perhaps even finally by God's choosing that man can know God.

As we survey the earthly life of King Jesus, we immediately see that Jesus chose twelve men to be "with Him." In the same way that God walked with Adam at creation in the cool of the day, Jesus walked with His chosen ones. While this walk was one of friendship, teaching, and ministry together, it was also a walk of revelation. Beyond these important realities we discover the ultimate purpose of this divine/human encounter. The mystical union of God and man is the ultimate purpose for which Jesus died on the cross. God and man who were once separated by sin are reconciled as one. Where there was separation, there is now unity and oneness.

Before we can explore the depths of the mystery of the union of God and man, we must first understand the criteria which God uses to choose His friends. At best this attempt to peer into the heart of God is a beginning. It would take eternity to understand the ways and choices of God. Even a dynamic personal relationship with Him yields only a little insight into His ways while we are yet in this world. With this honest assessment of our human limitations, we can try to begin to describe some that the Lord has chosen.

The Lord has chosen people who in some way are like Him. Simply stated, God has chosen the godly. However linguists define the term "godly," perhaps we can see the reflection or the likeness of God more clearly in the godly man than in the masses who are also made in His image. As we look at the man whom God has chosen, it is important to remember that God is always the initiator of this relationship. In the words of Jesus, "You did not choose Me, but I chose you" (John 15:16). Essentially, God sees something in the godly man which looks like Him and attracts Him to the one He made as His true child.

The first defining attribute of the man that He has chosen is an ability to "hear." When God chooses someone to be His friend, His "call" must first be heard. As noted earlier, King Jesus uses the illustration of a shepherd with His sheep to differentiate His own from the many. In a similar way the infant child recognizes the voice of mother or father as a primary means of identification and comfort. The ability to hear spiritually allows a communication between God and His people that separates them from the others of the world. This spiritual hearing is underscored in the personal "callings" of such great heroes of the faith like Abraham, Samuel, Moses, and Paul. The symbolic picture of a blaring trumpet is often used in the Bible to portray the call of God to those who are His. Moses, the man of God, speaks to the people of God with these famous words, "Hear, O Israel!" (Deut. 6:4). A hearing spiritual ear is depicted as the necessity for spiritual life and health. It is often the beginning point from which all else follows.

When God speaks through the prophet Isaiah about a people who should be His, we see a condition that is very sad:

> *"Go to this people and say,*
> *You will keep on hearing but you will not understand,*
> *And you will keep on seeing but will not perceive*
> *For the heart of this people has become dull*
> *And with their ears they scarcely hear*
> *And they have closed their eyes*
> *Otherwise they might see with their eyes*
> *And hear with their ears*
> *And understand with their heart*
> *And return and I would heal them."*

This passage, taken from Isaiah chapter 6 is also quoted by Jesus in Mark 4:12 as well as by the apostle Paul in Acts 28:26-27. In these passages, we see the essential quality of the ability to hear spiritually as directly related to the other blessings of God. We also read that hearing is connected with two other traits commonly found in godly men and women. Perhaps this is the reason that the Scripture exhorts us frequently, "Let those who have ears hear."

The ability to spiritually "see" also sets the godly man apart from many. Spiritual sight seems to be a common quality among the "set apart" ones that takes several different forms. For some like Abraham, spiritual sight was often equated with faith. When God told him to look upon the stars of Heaven, a promise was given him that by faith, his descendants would be more numerous than the stars. Abraham "believed God and it was reckoned to him as righteousness" (Galatians 4:3). The story of Abraham is a record of a man who could "see with his spiritual eyes" before things were manifested to his natural physical eyes. God has repeatedly chosen men and women who could see by the eye of faith to accomplish great things and demonstrate His own faithfulness. Many of these faith heroes are spoken of in the eleventh chapter of the book of Hebrews.

Another form of spiritual sight which marks the godly man is seen in the life of the prophet Elisha. We see the great man of God surrounded by an enemy army in Second Kings chapter 6. Elisha's servant responds to the impending assault with fear and uncertainty until his eyes are supernaturally opened by the Lord. Once his spiritual eyes are opened, he sees horses and chariots of fire around Elisha. The angelic warrior host outnumbers the naturally visible enemy army. It seems that Elisha must have "seen" this host all along. Spiritual sight in this setting is the ability "to see" into realm of the Spirit. John the Revelator was "in the spirit on the Lord's day" (Rev. 1:10) when he heard and "turned to see the voice that was speaking with me" (Rev. 1:12). The progression of "hearing and seeing" into the spirit realm is not only at the heart of John's revelation, but evidenced in the life of others such as Daniel, Ezekiel, Isaiah, and Paul. While not everyone that God has chosen experiences dreams or visions, there is a type of spiritual sight that is common among the godly ones He has chosen for Himself.

The final trait that seems most typical among the godly is a "heart for God." When the term "heart" is used here it refers not to the physical heart but to the inner part of a man that seems to respond positively to the Lord. As we look through the scriptures at men and woman that God chose for His purposes, the heart "after God" or "for God" or "toward God" is a common trait among the godly. Before the Lord set David on His kingly throne, He first looked at David's heart. The Bible tells us that the Lord was not looking at outward physical traits in the decision making process. God seemed to be impressed only by the inner man. "The Lord has sought out for Himself a man after His own heart, and the Lord has appointed Him as ruler over His people" (1 Samuel 13:14).

Throughout the scriptures, God seems to be looking for the heart which is inclined toward Him. It is as if the Lord seeks those who are moved with the same purpose, passions, and even similar values to His own.

God seems to choose those with a quality of character that is like His own. The heart matters to God and it matters most when it comes to being pliable in the hands of the Creator.

When the Lord looks at the masses, He always speaks to the need for a change of heart. This idea of a heart change among sinners is a very prevalent Bible theme. God addresses those whom their "heart is far from Me" through many of the prophets (see Matt. 15:8). In Jeremiah, He promises a new day when He will make an everlasting covenant with them. God said, "I will not turn away from them, to do them good; and I will put the fear [respect/reverence] of Me in their hearts so that they will not turn away from Me" (Jeremiah 32:40). This follows His promise to "put My law within them" and "on their heart I will write it; and I will be their God, and they shall be My people" (Jeremiah 31:33). It is readily evident that God is looking for an inner quality that respects Him and delights to do what pleases Him. God is looking for a heart inclined toward Him.

The heart after God is such a defining quality that it seems that a person cannot be godly without it. David cried out, "Create in me a clean heart, O God, and renew a right spirit in me" (Psalm 51:10). Jesus told His followers that it was not what entered them that defiled them, but rather the things that "come from the heart" (see Matt. 15:18). Jesus repeatedly rebuked unbelievers and even His own disciples for "hardness of heart" that caused spiritual blindness. (Mark 8:17-18). This great spiritual quality is identified for us in what Jesus calls the greatest commandment, "Love the Lord your God with all your heart, mind, soul, and strength" (Luke 10:27). The yielded heart is perhaps the most important asset for the godly man and for the Lord who gave man His spiritual heart.

In summary, we can see those things which make a man godly. The godly man loves God. The godly man is able to hear with spiritual ears when the Lord calls to Him. The godly man sees life through the eyes of faith. The godly man often sees into the realm of the Spirit to behold the life and activity of His God. Vision is his portion and action follows vision. The godly man's heart is "after God." The godly man will see and hear, but his love for God causes him to speak and act as the messenger of the Lord. Having seen and heard, he must speak. The godly man has been set apart for the Lord, and it cannot be kept a secret.

Now the mysteries of the hidden Kingdom unfold and demand an ongoing explanation and proclamation. When God has truly touched a man and claimed him for the Kingdom, there will be an impact and a sound which breaks forth from the Kingdom with a distinctive resonance that none can deny. The sound barriers will all be shattered when a godly man lays hold of the Kingdom. But before the noise starts, there must first be a union that will revolutionize our thinking.

CHAPTER 12

Mystical Union

Perhaps one of the greatest mysteries in the Kingdom of God is the phenomena of the union of God and man. This union is a mystical connection between God and man that is nothing less than perfection and fulfillment in pure spiritual consummation. It can be described as the joining of the Spirit of God with the human spirit to continually bring forth all the manifestations of abundant and eternal life. This heavenly life is primarily marked by peace, joy, and righteousness, though it has many expressions. Most assuredly, we are more likely to see the results of this mystical union than be able to adequately explain it. Nevertheless, we will try.

We have already seen that the Kingdom of God is essentially a Kingdom within the heart of man though it has many external expressions. This eternal and internal Kingdom is discovered in the context of a relationship with the Creator King. This Kingdom is both invisible yet visible to the eye of faith. It is a Heavenly Kingdom that is entered by faith in Jesus. In the Kingdom, Jesus is the door, the guide, the helper, and mans best friend. In essence, Jesus becomes the life of every believing man, woman, boy, and girl.

The new life that lives in the Kingdom realm comes through a *new birth* type of experience. At this new birth, a new man is born that is truly alive in the spirit and alive in God. This new man is a spirit being with a life that is eternal. He is a union of the faith and will of man with the eternal seed of the imperishable Word of God. The great teacher Paul said, "But he who is joined to the Lord is one spirit with Him" (1 Cor. 6:17).

Another way to say this is that a spirit-born man functions as one with the Lord just as a married couple functions as one. Physical union is only an expression of a higher order of unity depicting God's goal of oneness for man with God. The union of God and man is a living of God's life inside a man expressed outwardly through the life of the man. God is on the inside while the man is expressing God on the outside. This is the union that is truly a new creation as man takes on the purposes of God, the desires of God, and the character traits of God. The maturing spiritual man develops these qualities given by the eternal One who fathered him and gave him life. He no longer lives a life apart from God with selfish motives or independent attitudes. The spiritual man is a godly man that sets his mind on the things which are above the purely natural realm. This man lives and moves and finds his being in God. (See Acts 17:28.)

The mystical union is not simply about becoming a new creation man but finally about what God is able to produce in us and through us. His life in us is the substance and the ability to reproduce what is truly like Him. The born-again man becomes the vessel through whom God makes more of what He is. The man is the vessel, the life is God. Man is not absorbed into God, but becomes the building in which God chooses to display His greatness. Paul, the teacher sent from God, describes the mystical union this way, "It is no longer I who live but Christ now lives in me; and the life which I now live in the flesh I live by faith in the Son of God, who loved me and gave Himself up for me" (Galatians 2:20 NKJV). God lives in born-again people that they might know Him and do the works of God. His Kingdom comes to earth as it is in Heaven when man allows that Kingdom to come out from within him. Outwardly the shape and size looks like us, but inwardly the life flowing comes from God.

The beautiful result of this Heavenly union depicts the depths of the heart of God. *Only a life that is shared is truly a life.* God has made the union possible, but He has continued to give man the choice to fulfill His eternal plan. Those who enter this wonderful life experience the very life of God. God's life is a life without end, an abundant and eternal life. Knowing Him is eternal life. (See John 17:3.) This is the life that God intended for everyone. If only all would choose to enter in!

The final result of this mystical union between God and man is fruitfulness. When God lives His life out through a man there is reproduction of what He is. Those things that make Him God are multiplied in those who receive His life. God is seen working through the life of the man yielded to Him. The new creation man allows the life of God to touch His creation over and over through unselfish acts of love and kindness. In some measure, God repeatedly wraps Himself in the flesh of those who give themselves to Him for His purposes. While he is surely Omnipresent, He lives in those who live in Him. In this marvelous and mystical union there is satisfaction, meaning, and ongoing life. The union of God and man brings life. He is life. He continues to create more and more of what He is. This is certainly a wonderful way that God has chosen to express Himself!

CHAPTER 13

The Man Is the Message

There are tremendous spiritual truths that are logical results of the mystical union of God and man. One of the most powerful results of this mystical union is the way in which a man becomes the message of God to the world. It is all part of the journey.

When God chose to reveal Himself to the world in a definite way, He wrapped Himself in flesh and spoke to the world as Jesus the Christ. John said it this way in the Bible, "The Word became flesh, and dwelt among us... full of grace and truth" (John 1:14). Jesus is the statement or message of God to the world. The writer of the Book of Hebrews says it like this, "God who spoke in diverse ways in times past to the fathers, in these last days has spoken to us in the Son [Jesus]" (see Hebrews 1:1-2). In simple terms, the Son who came forth from His Heavenly Father revealed the nature of the invisible God. In the words of Jesus, "if you have seen Me, you have seen [God] My Father" (John 14:9). The message of God came as a man in Jesus. In Jesus, the fullness of the Godhead dwelt bodily. (See Colossians 1:19.) God is still speaking through Him today. Perhaps to the amazement of some, God continues to speak through other people as well that are united with Him.

The essential truth here is that the primary way God complements His written Word (the Bible) is with men and women who are living letters. These men and women who God has chosen to speak for Him illustrate the truths of God in their daily lives. This has always been true as prophets like Isaiah, Jeremiah, and Hosea were typical spokesmen for God as they illustrated the messages that God had given them with distinct actions. (See Isaiah 20:3, Jeremiah 13:1-11, and Hosea 1:2-9.) Those whom God has sent have always been His message to His people. The messages they spoke were almost always illustrated by the actions in their lives.

As the Word of God takes root in the heart of man, life is birthed and flows out of that man. The great preacher Paul said it this way, "You are the letter [message] of Christ, written not with ink but by the Spirit of the living God" (2 Cor. 3:3). It is readily evident that God has chosen to reveal Himself to men. It is also evident that God has chosen to reveal Himself through men. Those who know Christ personally and intimately not only have a revelation of God and Christ Jesus but become the revelation of God and Christ Jesus in the generation in which they live. The whole process of incarnation occurs repeatedly in some measure as we see God living His life out in a human vessel that houses a spirit-born man who is one with Christ. In this type of spiritual relationship, the man is the message sent from God.

Now having discussed this wonderful reality it is important to say that man does not become God nor is God a man as either me or you. While we are united with Him through His death and resurrection, we still remain distinct from Him. The married couple again serves as an effective illustration of this truth. While the two have become one in the sight of God, they are still both individuals and must choose daily to flow together in unity and harmony. Union is a choice that is made daily by the two that have become one. I believe this is what the apostle Paul meant when he said, "I die daily" (1 Cor. 15:31). He was speaking about a life joined to Christ that required a continual yielding to God and dying to His own self-preserving interests.

The people who are joined to Jesus become part of the Body of Christ. The Body of Christ is just another name for His Church. The Bible tells us that Jesus is the head of His Body which is the Church (see Colossians 1:18 and First Corinthians 12:12-27). The people of God must allow Jesus who is the head of His Body to lead them as they love, serve, and give of themselves. In this way, the Church which is the Body of Christ lives in the earth today and acts on behalf of King Jesus Christ the head.

Some have misunderstood this great mystery, but we simply want to emphasize the powerful way that God showed His love for the world through those who have been joined together with Him. God is able to express Himself and live out His life by blessing others through those who are willing to love and serve.

The speaking God uses men to preach or tell His story by their words and their works. The deeds are proof that the words are true. And with this revelation, we see why men must speak for God. While this is not the only way that God speaks, His Word needs a preacher. The preacher must be sent by God. The preacher is the vessel God has chosen. The preacher will speak with His mouth and with His life. Together the mouth and the life tell the story. It doesn't matter whether we like this fact. The truth is that the man is the message!

It may seem strange to us that God has chosen frail and feeble men and women to house the treasure of His Kingdom. The Bible says that we have this treasure in jars of clay or earthen vessels. (See 2 Corinthians 4:7.) The majesty and wisdom of God is displayed in the contents of the vessel as well as the vessel itself. The Creator demonstrates the magnificence of His creation and love for diversity as He makes all of us unique in our own way. Once again the Creator who is Wisdom personified, is vindicated by all of the children that He has created. (See Luke 7:35.) If we truly have eyes to see the image of God in every man, we will say with the Scripture, "He has made everything beautiful in its time" (Eccles. 3:11 NIV). To God, all of His children must certainly be beautiful. In keeping with our overall discussion, all of the children of God are speaking in some way for Him with their lives as well as their words. By the wisdom of God we can understand the hidden things of the spirit which are being spoken through the lives of those who know their heavenly Father. If the eyes of our hearts have truly been enlightened, we will also understand the people who are separated from God by sin and selfishness. Ultimately, we all need to know that each of us will give an account for the message that we are sending with our lives.

CHAPTER 14

Tellers of the Truth

Throughout history men have encountered the living God. The simple reason for this is that God wants to be known. While these encounters vary in type and intensity, the usual result in man is change. The other result is frequently proclamation. While there are times that God silenced the man whom He meets, most Heavenly encounters turn even the most timid person into a teller of truth.

An experience with God often produces a response or a reaction in man. When Jeremiah the prophet heard the words of God he described it as "fire shut up in my bones" (Jeremiah 20:9). After Mary had seen the resurrected Jesus outside an empty tomb, she immediately went and declared to His friends, "I have seen the Lord!" (John 20:18). Paul who had once persecuted the followers of Jesus had a powerful life-changing encounter with the risen Jesus. As he was traveling, "a light from Heaven flashed around him and he fell to the ground and heard a voice" (Acts 9:3-4). Paul's dramatic encounter with Jesus had predictable results, "immediately he began to proclaim Jesus" (Acts 9:20). Time after time the story line is the same. The people who have heard or seen, became people who must tell. This Kingdom reality is rooted in the revelation that God wants to be known and He does nothing "unless He reveals His secret counsel to His servants the prophets" (Amos 3:7). The most elementary understanding of this could be called show-and-tell. In simple but theological terms, the result of revelation is communication.

The amazing truth in all this is that God uses men and women to proclaim who He is. But even beyond this great revelation, the proclamation of God is not limited to godly men and women or even to the human race. All creation tells of the Heavenly King and His hidden Kingdom. The Bible is full of occasions where angels who were created by God tell of His excellent greatness. At the birth of Jesus, angels said, "Glory to God in the highest and on earth peace among men with whom He is pleased" (Luke 2:14). Songs in the Bible like Psalm 19 record these words, "The Heavens are telling of the glory of God and their expanse is declaring the work of His hands. Day to day pours forth speech and night reveals knowledge" (Psalm 19:12). All creation declares His mighty works.

The reality and revelation of God is so powerful that it seems to demand a joyful telling by His creation. This is the truth that Jesus declared when He rode triumphantly into Jerusalem before His crucifixion. When the masses recognized the coming of their awaited King, many began to shout and praise God. In the background, some critics grumbled so Jesus told them, "If these [people] become silent, the stones will cry out!" (Luke 19:40). In a world of critics, complainers, and counterfeits, the truth is still the truth. Revelation demands communication, and all creation declares His glorious Kingdom. That will always be good news!

CHAPTER 15

Granted

As we ponder the process that accompanies the inward journey, we are sometimes surprised by the way people react to the mysteries of the Kingdom. Obviously some people seem to be more receptive and aware of Kingdom realities than others. At the same time, many folks seem to go through life without really understanding much of anything beyond their own little worlds. What is it that separates those who see from those who fail to see? Why is understanding given to some travelers and not to others? Only Jesus can give us the answer.

The public ministry of Jesus lasted about three years. During this time of teaching and working miracles, Jesus selected twelve men to be His inner circle. The twelve learned His message and His methods as they traveled with Him and helped with the work. It was their privilege to experience a special depth of revelation that came with their special relationship to Jesus. While the message of the Kingdom of God was declared to the multitude, only a few were given the keys to understanding the Kingdom.

After one particular teaching session about a man who sowed seed, Jesus told His closest friends a secret about the Kingdom. While the masses heard only a parable about a man and His seed, Jesus gave His closest friends a full explanation of the meaning of the parable. As Jesus spoke to His inner circle, He repeatedly used the phrase "unto you it has been granted to know the mystery of the Kingdom of God" (Mark 4:13). Here in the passage of biblical record we discover the explanation for the revelation. Simply, God can be known because He has chosen to reveal Himself. Revelation is a gift from God to man. The mysteries of the Kingdom of God are revealed to man by virtue of the kind and benevolent nature of God who chooses to be known. No one can discover God unless God chooses to bestow the gift of revelation upon that person. The privilege of providence is to declare, "To you it has been granted."

The focus of this journey has primarily been on the revelation of the Kingdom of God as revealed through relationship with Jesus. We have come to understand that without a revelation from God, we can really know little or nothing about Him. Revelation is a gift of God to those He has chosen. Jesus emphasized this truth when He said, "a man can receive nothing unless it is given to Him from Heaven" (John 3:27). Revelation is a privilege. The consummate revelation of God is in Jesus who is called the Christ. We can say with the Bible, "in Christ Jesus are hidden all the treasures of wisdom and knowledge..." (see Colossians 2:2-3). He is, essentially, His own gift to us. He gives us Himself, and only then can we know Him as we receive Him gladly.

Jesus is the indescribable great gift of God. He is the goal and the reward and the treasure of the hidden realm of the Kingdom. He is the personification of all that is good and pure. Jesus is the revelation of God in human form. All that the other world of God's Kingdom includes can be seen in the man Jesus as he serves among the people of the earth. He is life and His life is available to us. This is the crowning reality of the Kingdom of God. As we partake of His life we move into the realm of His Kingdom to rule over every other lower thing as kings with Him. As joint heirs of the Kingdom, we are made to be a Kingdom of priests. We are to be those who serve Him and serve among the people as those who display His nature and His ways. We are to act with the authority that has been issued to us from the Kingdom of God. We are to honor Him as seasoned travelers who have ventured into the world of the spirit. We declare Him to be the King of Kings as we rule over our fleshly desires and yield to His ultimate authority in our lives. Even death must bow before His Kingly rule. Nothing can conquer this King of all kings. All the mysteries of the Kingdom are wrapped up in the King. As we know Him, we shall surely know all the mysteries of His Kingdom!

While there are yet many other mysteries of the Kingdom to explore, this concludes the most important phase of our journey into the hidden world of His Kingdom. As the Lord gives us more, we will gladly share it with those who will hear. Until then, we thank the Lord for what He has shown us. Our prayer for each one is quite simple: May revelation be your portion.

May proclamation be your profession. May praise be your position, and may Jesus always be your King!

Your fellow traveler,
Mark Van Deman

An Explorer's Manual for Navigating the Hidden World

The purpose of this study guide is to assist the spiritual traveler and/or student in understanding the source of the truths that are declared in this book. The chapter-by-chapter guide brings an emphasis to the questions which are central to the ideas presented by the author in each chapter.

Many of the questions will include references to the Bible to aid the traveler in an overall understanding of the truth. These Bible references are not meant to always be a direct answer to the questions for discussion. The purpose of including the Bible references is simply to help the spiritual traveler formulate an accurate view of the larger concepts being discussed by the author.

When a Scripture reference seems unclear, vague, or obscure, it should be considered in light of the overall discussion within the chapter and the book, and not specifically as related to just one particular question. The goal of the author in developing this study guide is to simply facilitate a deeper journey and experience in the Kingdom of God.

The study guide is designed for individual study or small group use. It naturally lends itself to 15 sessions or 15 weeks. There is no specific time limit imposed on the traveler, but it is helpful to move through the book with a goal for completion in mind.

If the study guide is used in the small group setting, it can easily be self-directed without a trained leader. When a Christian worker leads a study of the material in this book, it is suggested that all participants be allowed to explore a variety of insights and ideas as the truths of the Bible unfold. Truth is relational and best realized in a positive and encouraging learning environment. A rigid, inflexible approach is usually unproductive.

While any translation of the Bible is useful for understanding spiritual realities, the author utilizes primarily the updated New American Standard Bible, or in some cases, the King James Version. Additional references can be helpful, but it is not necessary for the student to know the original Bible languages in order to understand the Kingdom of God.

The spiritual traveler is encouraged to take notes and write down other questions as they arise during the study of the Kingdom of God. The journey is not to be made hastily or insincerely when the destination is the Kingdom of God. This is the most important journey any of us will ever take as we venture into the hidden realm of the spirit. Let us enter with expectation and awe as we discover the purposes for which we were made.

Your fellow traveler,
Mark Van Deman

CHAPTER 1

The Other World

WHAT DIFFERENCE DOES IT MAKE THAT ANOTHER HIDDEN WORLD EXISTS?

The hidden world of the spirit is the only true eternal world. Everything in this present world is passing away, but the hidden realm of the spirit lasts forever. For this reason alone, entrance into the hidden realm of the spirit is literally a life and death matter. The hidden realm of the spirit encompasses a world that has no beginning and knows no end. Everything in this world is brimming with life. It is a world where sickness, disease, and sorrow can not survive. Even death itself is without power in this hidden world. Those who enter live, while those who are outside of the hidden realm of the spirit never taste true life.

This heavenly realm is a perfect world, for it is the world that God lives in. Seasoned travelers will agree that the discovery of this hidden world is among the most important discoveries a person can make while they are on planet earth. Perhaps this is the reason that the greatest man to ever live said, "Seek first His Kingdom and His righteousness, and all these other things shall be added to you." (REFERENCES: MATTHEW 6:19-33, 1 CORINTHIANS 2:6-16, REVELATION 22:1-17)

What is the difference between exploring concepts about the Kingdom of God and potentially experiencing it as a reality?

Why would the author emphasize the difference in these two aspects of His purpose for writing the book?

What is the ultimate goal that the author seeks?

How would you describe a Kingdom in your own words?

Is there a connection between the King and His Kingdom?
(JOHN 18:36) (MATTHEW 12:28)

Who is the king that the author is writing about?
(MATTHEW 21:5-11) (REVELATION 19:11-16)

How is a king different from an elected official?
(DANIEL 6:15) (MATTHEW 28:18)

What difference does it make that God is a King and not an elected official?
(ECCLESIASTES 8:4) (DANIEL 4:17)

How should people in a Kingdom respond to the words and actions of their king?
(1 TIMOTHY 2:1-4) (ESTHER 1:10-21)

Why is the Kingdom of God a mystery to many people?
(MARK 4:11-12) (LUKE 8:4-10)

Where does the Bible say that Jesus came from?
(JOHN 6:51) (JOHN 1:1-2) (JOHN 16:28)

What qualifies Jesus to be the interpreter of the hidden Kingdom?
(JOHN 5:19) (JOHN 6:36-47)

What is the value of having a guide or interpreter as we enter a new country or Kingdom?

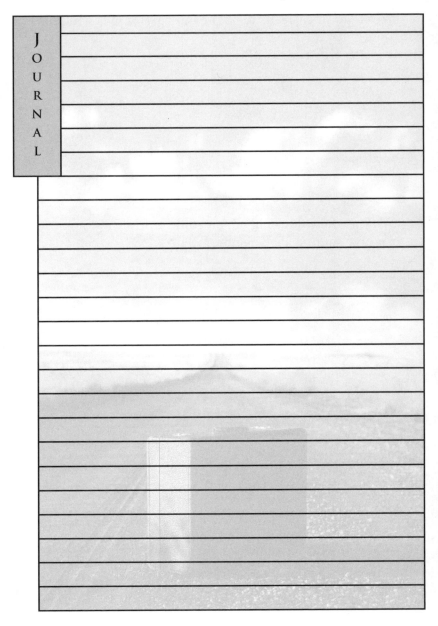

JOURNAL

THE OTHER WORLD

A Traveler's Guide to the Spirit Realm

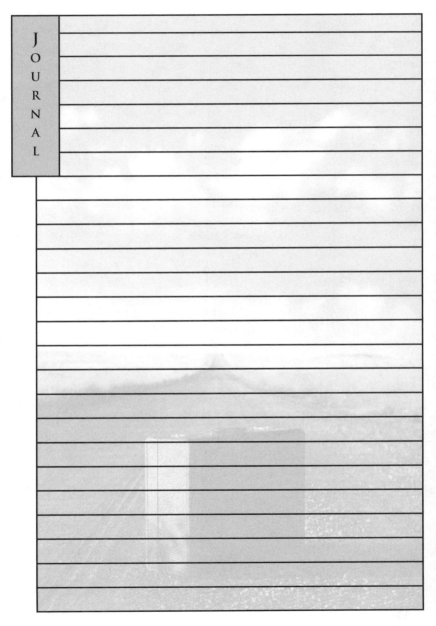

JOURNAL

CHAPTER 2

The Way In

HOW DOES A PERSON DISCOVER THE HIDDEN REALM OF THE SPIRIT?

An individual discovers the hidden world when the door to this wonderful Kingdom is opened by the King of the eternal world. The King issues an invitation to the traveler which may come in a variety of forms. Normally this invitation is impressed upon the mind and spirit of a traveler to consider the possibilities of an unseen world. The King may choose to deliver the invitation through a messenger or he may deliver the invitation personally. Either way, the invitation arrives with a simple message: Come.

Upon receipt of the invitation, the spiritual sojourner enters through a specific door and proceeds through a well-defined process which has been designed by the King. The entrance process requires a seasoned guide (Jesus), an appropriate attitude (humility), and a decided willingness to follow. The way is well marked and lighted with the light of Life.

As soon as the spiritual traveler submits to this process and protocol of the Kingdom, the spiritual adventure truly begins. Desire and determination normally affect the pace at which the journey progresses, while love determines the destination. A traveler who hungers and thirsts for a true relationship with the King of the Kingdom will be well-satisfied on the journey. This spiritual hunger and thirst is rewarded with fulfillment and other new opportunities for spiritual discovery. Once the journey begins, there is no limit to the possibility of exploration or discovery because the hidden Kingdom is a world without end.

(REFERENCES: MATTHEW 5:3, MARK 1:14-19, GALATIANS 1:11-24, MATTHEW 11:25-30)

THE WAY IN

Have you ever experienced a "yearning deep within" that the author is writing about?
(PSALM 42:1-7) (LUKE 14:27-32)

Did you wish that you could meet someone who could lead you into all truth?
(JOHN 14:6) (JOHN 16:13-15)

Why would a person need the help of a guide when they are on a journey or expedition?
(PSALM 31:3) (PSALM 32:8) (JOHN 14:3-5)

Why do we need a guide to enter the hidden world of the Kingdom of God?
(JOHN 3:11-13) (JOHN 14:6)

How does the "protocol" of the Kingdom determine access into the Kingdom?
(JOHN 3:27) (LUKE 18:17) (JAMES 4:6)

Why does a person need a personal invitation to enter the Kingdom of God?
(ISAIAH 55:1-4) (MATTHEW 11:28-30) (REVELATION 22:17)

Is it possible for a person to hear the invitation of the King within his inner man, or will this only be made known as he starts seeking?
(ISAIAH 33:13) (ISAIAH 55:6) (JOHN 10:2-6) (MATTHEW 6:33)

THE WAY IN

To what extent does desire determine access to the Kingdom of God?
(PSALM 37:4) (JEREMIAH 29:13) (MATTHEW 5:6)

What evidence is there inside you that you want to enter the Kingdom of God?
(MATTHEW 7:16-23)

JOURNAL

JOURNAL

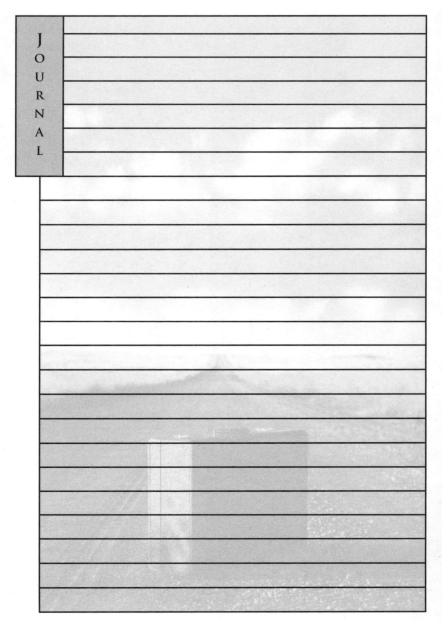

JOURNAL

CHAPTER 3

Through the Door

WHAT KEY DECISIONS MUST BE MADE IN ORDER TO
ENTER THE HIDDEN REALM OF THE KINGDOM OF GOD?

The first key decision a spiritual traveler makes is related to the invitation to enter the Kingdom. A wise traveler will respond to the invitation to come into the Kingdom. He will understand the value of a seasoned guide and rely on Jesus to lead him into the hidden realm of the Kingdom of life. This first step into the hidden world requires a step of faith. The traveler must trust the voice, the invitation, and the guide. Unless a person trusts Jesus and believes He is willing and able to lead him into life, he will never enter the Kingdom.

The second key decision a person must make who enters the hidden Kingdom requires a change in the person. The spiritual traveler must consent to being changed at the very core of His being in order to live and move and breathe in the hidden world. A process of total transformation will ultimately take place on the inside of the traveler which will enable him or her to experience the fullness of the Kingdom. The most interesting thing about the change is that it is both a process and an instantaneous event. Most theologians call this change conversion, while spiritual travelers understand it as life.

(REFERENCES: JOHN 3:36, JOHN 10:1-11, JOHN 14:6, REVELATION 22:17)

Why would the Kingdom have a door through which people must enter?

How is Jesus the only door into the Kingdom of God? (JOHN 10:1-9)

In what ways is entrance into the Kingdom of God both easy and difficult?
(MATTHEW 5:13) (ROMANS 10:13)

What does it mean to be converted?
(ISAIAH 55:7) (ACTS 26:18)

How do people become like little children in the conversion process?
(MATTHEW 18:2-4)

Who is in control of the child of God?
(ROMANS 8:12-14) (GALATIANS 2:20) (1 CORINTHIANS 6:20)
(COLOSSIANS 3:15)

How can a person relinquish control of his/her life to God?
(PSALM 37:3-6) (ISAIAH 55:6-7) (MATTHEW 10:39) (1 PETER 5:7)

What does it mean to be born again?
(JOHN 3:6-9) (1 PETER 1:3-5)

Why is it difficult for some people to be "born again"?
(MARK 1:14-15) (MARK 10:13)

How is the "new birth" foundational to entering the Kingdom of God?
(ISAIAH 28:16) (JOHN 3:3-5)

What things happen when a person is born into the Kingdom of God?
(ROMANS 8: 15-16) (2 CORINTHIANS 5:17) (1 JOHN 5:10-12)

What inheritance is given to every citizen born into the Kingdom of God?
(1 CORINTHIANS 3:22) (EPHESIANS 1:3-14)

In what way is the child of God an heir to the wealth and treasure in the Kingdom?
(1 CORINTHIANS 3:21-23) (COLOSSIANS 2:2-3)

What steps does a person need to take to experience new birth and enter the Kingdom?
(JOHN 1:12) (ACTS 2:38-39) (ACTS 16:31)

How is new life the result of believing and receiving Jesus?
(JOHN 3:36) (JOHN 11:25) (ROMANS 10:8-10)

A Traveler's Guide to the Spirit Realm

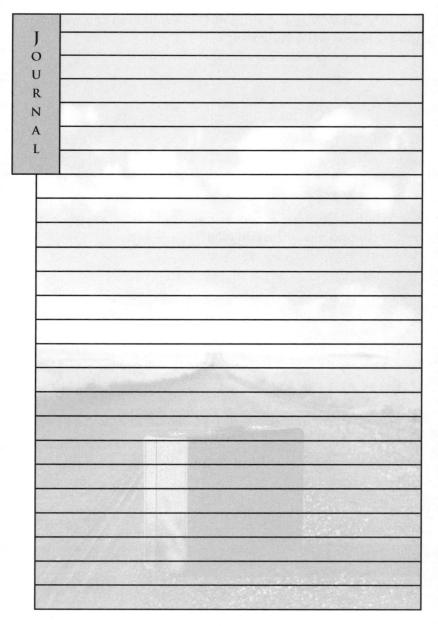

JOURNAL

Through the Door

J
O
U
R
N
A
L

The Treasure Within

WHAT IS THE "TREASURE WITHIN" THAT THE AUTHOR SPEAKS ABOUT?

The concept of a "treasure within" has layered meanings. First the treasure within speaks of a Kingdom that is literally located within the innermost being of the spiritual traveler. The Kingdom of Heaven exists on the inside of the spiritual man. This internal Kingdom is marked by spiritual seeing and hearing that both occur within his very spirit man. This Kingdom is not an external one, though it has numerous outward manifestations that indicate its substance and reality. These realities will normally take the form of peace, joy, and righteousness in the Spirit of God.

Second, the idea of a treasure within alludes to the central reality of the Kingdom which is unconditional perfect love. At the core of the Kingdom is the treasure of the King's amazing and unfathomable love for people. Everything within the Kingdom flows out of this central reality. Perfect love is the dominant force that shapes every other reality of the Kingdom. This love is so dynamic and overwhelming that the spiritual traveler will experience a great sense of wealth and beauty as he or she explores the vastness of this great Kingdom.

(REFERENCES: LUKE 17:20-21, JOHN 4:10-14, ROMANS 14:16)

As a child of God, what is the primary change that has occurred in your life?

(JOHN 9:25) (ROMANS 8:1) (COLOSSIANS 1:13)

What happens to the person when his/her spiritual eyes are first opened?

(MARK 2:12) (LUKE 5:25-26)

What do you see as a child of God that you could not see naturally?

(MARK 4:10-11) (JOHN 1:51A) (HEBREWS 2:9)

In what way does the child of God hear the voice of God in his inner being?

(JEREMIAH 7:23) (MATTHEW 7:24-27) (1 JOHN 3:19-22)

How is the Bible a primary source for hearing and seeing God?
(LUKE 8:18) (JOHN 17:17) (ROMANS 10:17) (2 TIMOTHY 3:16)

How is Jesus a good shepherd to the people of God?
(PSALM 23) (JOHN 10:11-15)

What does the author suggest is the greatest treasure in the Kingdom of God?
(ROMANS 8:38-39)

What imagery does the author use to describe the vastness of the love of God?
(EZEKIEL 47:1-12) (REVELATION 22:1)

Why would the author use many words to say that the love of God is unexplainable?
(JOHN 21:25) (2 CORINTHIANS 9:15)

How do you feel about being loved by God, and why does God love people so much?
(JAMES 1:17-18) (1 JOHN 4:16)

When you experience the love of God, what does it make you want to say and do?
(ROMANS 1:14-15) (1 JOHN 4:7-8) (1 JOHN 4:19)

THE TREASURE WITHIN

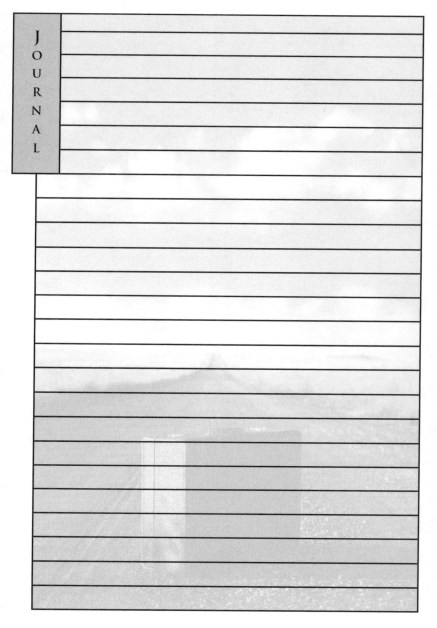

JOURNAL

CHAPTER 5

The Treasure in Him

HOW IS THE TREASURE OF THE KINGDOM HIDDEN IN GOD?

The natural visible world and the unseen world of the spirit are both expressions of who God is. Everything that exists expresses God in same way. His unseen attributes and nature are made known through creation. It simply takes revelation and wisdom to see where His hand has shaped all that is made. Sojourners that travel into the hidden realm of the spirit will discover that God the king is the source of all things. As the source of all things, He is perfect in all His ways. This perfection is discovered through a personal relationship with Him.

He is the great treasure hidden in His own eternal Kingdom. Travelers discover that He is nothing less than perfect love. His perfect love is revealed in Jesus. Everything that can be seen or known about God is revealed in a dynamic relationship with Jesus. In Him we discover that the treasures of Heaven are not far off, but are accessible to all those who know and love Him. Jesus is the revealer of all truth. He is the revealer of the hidden Kingdom. Ultimately He is the consummate revelation of God.

(REFERENCES: ROMANS 1:20, JOHN 1:14, JOHN 3:16, COLOSSIANS 2:1-7)

Why would the King choose to be our personal guide into His invisible Kingdom?
(MARK 6:33-34) (JOHN 14:6)

What discovery do we make about the nature of the Kingdom as we explore it with Jesus?
(LUKE 17:20) (1 CORINTHIANS 15:50)

Where is the Kingdom of God located?
(LUKE 17:21)

What are we learning about the King as He guides us through His Kingdom?
(LUKE 12:32)

Why would the great King invite us into the realm of His life?
(JOHN 15:3-11)

How does the kindness of the King create a growing sense of gratitude in a child of God?
(LUKE 7:40-50) (ROMANS 2:4)

In what ways is the Heavenly King everything you had personally hoped for?
(SONG OF SOLOMON 5:10)

What is there about a Kingdom of love that makes us want to know more about it?
(ACTS 8:26-40)

What unusual wounds does the King bear in His body?
(ISAIAH 53:5) (JOHN 19:34) (JOHN 20:27)

How does the King wear His scars?
(COLOSSIANS 2:13-15) (HEBREWS 2:9-10)

JOURNAL

A Traveler's Guide to the Spirit Realm

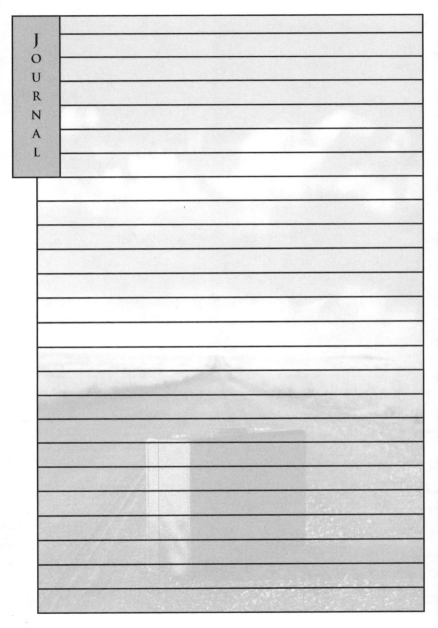

JOURNAL

CHAPTER 6

Colliding Kingdoms

WHAT CAUSED THE COLLISION OF THE TWO WORLDS?

The Kingdom of God collided with the earthly visible world when man chose to set up a competing Kingdom with a competing ruler king. In essence, man chose to depose God as true king over all in an attempt to become the ruler of this present world. Man's choice to be his own king and to go his own way was rooted in selfishness. Theologians say that sin entered the world inasmuch as friendship and fellowship with God was broken. Life at its core was tainted by sin and selfishness. The tragic final result of this rebellion was that life itself was terminated. Death entered the world through sin and spread to all men as the horrible consequence of separation between man and God.

From that time forward, the fallen world of man has continued to collide with the life of God and His Kingdom of perfect love. These two worlds are perpetually at war for the hearts and souls of men. The King of Love calls for men to forsake sin and selfishness, follow Him, and live eternally in the Kingdom of God. At the same time, self-seeking man is lured to stay in the natural realm of darkness where sin and death remain. Sadly, many people choose darkness because their deeds are evil and their hearts are far from God. Spiritual blindness keeps them in darkness because they do not receive Jesus who is the one who comes to bring light and life to a sinful world.

A Traveler's Guide to the Spirit Realm

(REFERENCES: ROMANS 3:10-18, ROMANS 5:12, GALATIANS 5:17-24, EPHESIANS 6:12-13)

In what book is the mystery of the scars revealed?
(PSALM 40:7) (JOHN 17:17)

What was the simple desire of the Creator according to the book where the story about the King and His scars are explained?
(GENESIS 3:8) (JOHN 17:21)

The selfish choices of man brought about what ultimate consequences?
(GENESIS 3:16-22) (ROMANS 5:12)

How do people become opponents of the King and His eternal Kingdom?
(ISAIAH 53:6) (JEREMIAH 5:23-25) (PHILIPPIANS 3:18-19)

In what way does the kingdom of a selfish and self-centered man collide with the perfect and eternal Kingdom of God?
(ROMANS 8:7) (GALATIANS 5:17) (2 THESSALONIANS 2:3-10)

Who can bridge the gap between fallen men in his fallen world with the Kingdom of God?
(MATTHEW 1:19-21)

Why would the King want to save the human race?
(PSALM 100:3) (JOHN 3:16)

How does the King choose to enter human history?
(LUKE 1:26-28)

What is the mission of the Creator King as He wraps Himself in flesh?
(ROMANS 6:22) (1 JOHN 3:5-9)

What are five things we see in the human life of Jesus while He is on the earth?
(JOHN 14:8-9) (HEBREWS 1:1-3)

Who are the foes that Jesus will conquer as He invades this fallen order?
(1 CORINTHIANS 15:53-57)

What does the author mean when he uses the term "love personified" to speak of Jesus?
(JOHN 1:14) (1 JOHN 1:1-3)

JOURNAL

COLLIDING KINGDOMS

J
O
U
R
N
A
L

CHAPTER 7

The Cross

WHY DID JESUS DIE ON THE CROSS?

Mankind has always been loved by God but became separated from Him by sin. While a perfect and holy God longed for reconciliation with man, the resulting severity of sin's consequence was death. At the beginning of creation God had declared that there would be no forgiveness or remission of sin without the shedding of blood. Life is in the blood. No animal blood could bring life to man. Only a man could die for man. The only man capable of bridging the gap between fallen man and perfect God was the God/man Jesus.

The sinless man Jesus was born from above and carried the untainted blood of His Father God. His holy blood was shed on the Cross for the forgiveness of sins for all mankind. He was the perfect sacrifice for the sins of the world. Simultaneously, He was both Just and the Justifier of man. He gave Himself to reconcile God and man. At the Cross, the gift of life flowed out of death to give life to everyone that would receive Him.

(**REFERENCES:** ROMANS 5:6-8, GALATIANS 3:13-14, 2 CORINTHIANS 5:18-21, HEBREWS 9:11-22)

The Cross was devised by Romans for what purpose?
(MARK 15:22-39)

How is the Cross a place of Divine Justice?
(ROMANS 3:21-26) (ROMANS 5:18-19) (1 JOHN 2:2)

How is the Cross a place of infinite love?
(ROMANS 5:6-11) (ROMANS 5:14) (1 JOHN 4:9-14)

What natural things led to the crucifixion of Jesus?
(JOHN 5:8) (JOHN 11:19) (JOHN 12:42-43) (MATTHEW 26:14-15)

According to the Bible narrative, was the crucifixion of Jesus a mistake?
(MARK 8:31-34) (JOHN 1:29) (1 PETER 1:17-21) (REVELATION 13:8)

Who is the only perfect man that was capable of reconciling fallen man with God?
(HEBREWS 4:14-16) (HEBREWS 7:26-28)

What does the Bible mean when it says that the wages of sin are death?
(ISAIAH 59:2) (ROMANS 6:23)

How did Jesus pay the price for every man?
(MARK 10:45) (EPHESIANS 2:13) (1 TIMOTHY 2:6)

How would you describe the death of Jesus?
(ISAIAH 53) (LUKE 23:33-56) (JOHN 19:1-30)

Is there anyone that Jesus didn't die for?
(ACTS 10:34) (2 CORINTHIANS 5:14-15) (TITUS 2:11)

Who knew what would happen three days after the crucifixion of Jesus?
(LUKE 24:1-9) (1 TIMOTHY 3:16)

THE CROSS

JOURNAL

Up From the Grave

IN WHAT WAY IS THE RESURRECTION ESSENTIAL TO THE KINGDOM OF GOD?

If there is no resurrection from the dead, there is no proof that life triumphs over death. The resurrection of Jesus is the proof that life triumphs over death. The resurrection of Jesus is also evidence that sins were forgiven at the Cross. The resurrection of Jesus validates His claims that He was sent from God and had authority to forgive sins.

Without the death and resurrection of Jesus, mankind is still separated from God and dead in its sin. The beauty of the resurrection is that it opens the door to life. It is nothing less than the gateway to the hidden realm of God's Kingdom. The resurrection makes life possible for every man as it proves that life is more powerful than death.

The resurrection also attests to the perfect loving character of God. When there was a great separation with man, He made the way for reconciliation possible. He made a relationship possible that otherwise would have been impossible. The spiritual traveler must understand that there is no reconciliation with resurrection. Ultimately the resurrection of Jesus is the essential cornerstone event in the Kingdom of God that is inseparable from the birth and sacrificial death of Jesus.

(REFERENCES: JOHN 11:25-26, 1 CORINTHIANS 15:3-58, HEBREWS 7:22-28)

What does the author mean by "the only way to truly live is to die first"?
(MARK 8:31-38) (LUKE 17:33)

Did Jesus know that He would die on a cross?
(LUKE 9:20-27) (LUKE 13:31-35) (LUKE 18:31-33)

In what way is the death of Jesus a ransom for those in slavery?
(JOB 33:23-24) (MATTHEW 20-28) (1 CORINTHIANS 6:20)

What did Jesus say about His life after death?
(MATTHEW 12:41) (MATTHEW 27:63) (LUKE 24:7)

Describe the amazing thing that happened to Jesus three days after He was crucified.
(MATTHEW 28:1-10) (MARK 16:1-8)

What right did Jesus give those who received Him?
(JOHN 1:12) (1 JOHN 3:1-3)

What was suddenly possible after the death and resurrection of Jesus?
(JOHN 15:15) (HEBREWS 4:14-16)

How did Jesus become the "reconciler" of man with God?
(ROMANS 5:10) (2 CORINTHIANS 5:18-21)

What happened historically and in all eternity that caused the door to the Kingdom of God to be opened for all who believed in Him?
(HEBREWS 9:11-15) (HEBREWS 10:19-23)

In what way does the Creator make relationship with Him possible?
(JOHN 1:29) (HEBREWS 7:19-25)

What is the promise to everyone who believes?
(ACTS 2:37-39) (GALATIANS 3:13-29) (2 TIMOTHY 1:1)

Does the King expect anything from us?
(JOHN 3:36) (JOHN 20:26-29) (1 JOHN 5:1-12)

What is the foundation for all life and truth according
to the Bible?
(ACTS 4:12) (ROMANS 1:4) (1 PETER 1:3-5)

A Traveler's Guide to the Spirit Realm

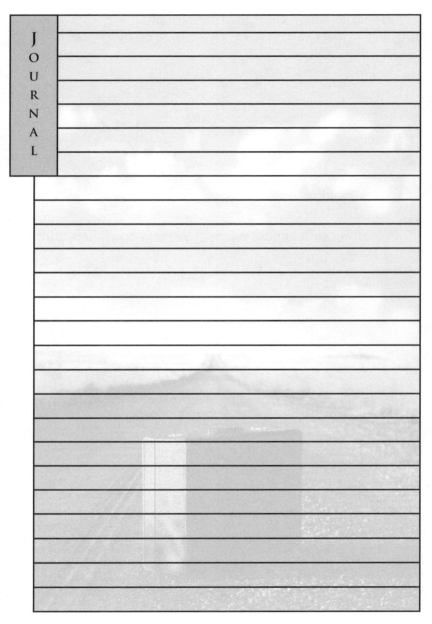

JOURNAL

JOURNAL

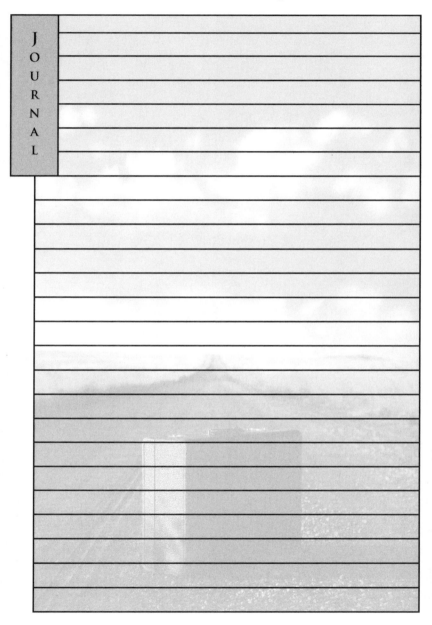

JOURNAL

CHAPTER 9

The King and the Kingdom

HOW DOES THE KINGDOM REVOLVE AROUND THE KING?

The Kingdom of God is the realm over which God the king rules. God's kingship, His authority, His order, His nature, His wisdom, and more are all expressed in His Kingdom. The way he relates to His Kingdom reflects His character and His purposes. His people are a vital part of His Kingdom. Their lives revolve around His life. A king must be king over someone and something. He is king over His people and over His Kingdom. The way in which he relates to His subjects is proof of the superiority of His Kingdom over all other Kingdoms. Even His citizens are subject to Him by their choice. Their allegiance to Him is evidence to the fact that He is worthy to be called the King of all Kings. The King is inseparable from His Kingdom. Everything in the Kingdom revolves around Him.

(REFERENCES: JOHN 18:36-37, HEBREWS 12:18-29, REVELATION 1:6, REVELATION 21-22)

How is the Kingdom connected to the King?
(MATTHEW 6:13) (LUKE 4:43) (LUKE 22:28-30)

What is the result of understanding the Kingdom?
(LUKE 13:18) (JOHN 1:17-18) (ACTS 17:28)

When does a follower of Jesus receive the life that He has promised?
(LUKE 19:1-10) (HEBREWS 4:6-8)

How near is the Kingdom of God?
(MATTHEW 4:17) (LUKE 17:21)

What does the evidence point to as the key to really experiencing life?
(JOHN 1: 3-4) (JOHN 8:12)

What did Jesus do throughout His ministry to verify the validity of His teaching?
(JOHN 20:30-31) (1 CORINTHIANS 4:20)

Why did Jesus teach primarily about the Kingdom of God after His resurrection?
(ACTS 1:3)

Why is Jesus called the King of kings?
(PHILIPPIANS 2:5-11) (1 TIMOTHY 6:15-16) (HEBREWS 1:8-9)

How long does the Bible teach that the Kingdom of Jesus will last?
(DANIEL 6:26) (LUKE 1:33) (HEBREWS 12:28)

Who is the Kingdom of Heaven prepared for?
(MATTHEW 25:19-34) (1 CORINTHIANS 2:9) (HEBREWS 11:13-16)

THE KING AND THE KINGDOM

A Traveler's Guide to the Spirit Realm

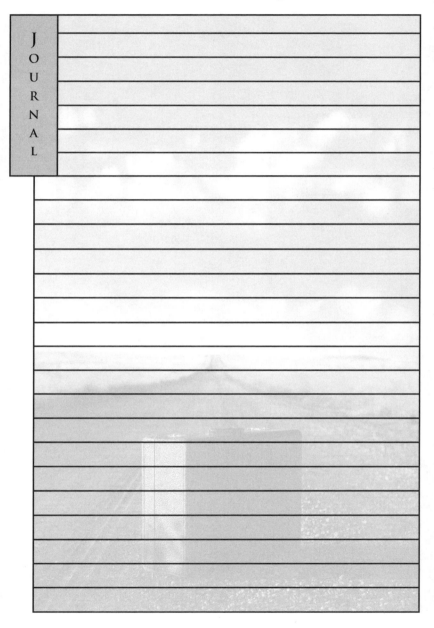

CHAPTER 10

Friends of the King

WHAT DOES IT MEAN TO BE A FRIEND OF GOD?

A friend of God is someone who knows God intimately and personally and can be trusted by God. This friendship is possible because God initiated the relationship. Spiritual travelers discover that God's desire for friendship is at the center of His purpose for sending Jesus into the world to die for the sins of man. A friend of God understands that God wants to share His world with us.

This shared world is grounded in a trusting relationship where God and man live peacefully and harmoniously together. This connection and oneness is demonstrated in a common sense of purpose with an agreement of values and a mutual desire for companionship. Eventually a friend of God is joined with God to work together with Him and share in His plans for Creation. In the final analysis, a friend of God shares the very life that God has given and gives it back as a gift of appreciation and love.

(REFERENCES: JOHN 14:23, JOHN 15:14-15, JOHN 17:1-26)

What is the ultimate desire of God?
(JOHN 15:14-16)

What is the greatest possible demonstration of love according to Jesus?
(JOHN 15:13)

In what way did Jesus demonstrate the greatness of His love?
(JOHN 17:19) (ROMANS 5:16)

Why would the King want to be friends with us?
(LUKE 7:34) (JOHN 17:19)

What is the most personal aspect of the fact that Jesus wants to be your friend?
(JOHN 15:14)

What kind of friend will Jesus be to you?
(PROVERBS 17:17) (JOHN 13:1) (HEBREWS 13:15)

How will you express your friendship with Jesus?
(JOHN 3:29-30) (JOHN 15:9-10) (JAMES 4:4)

Does God have a goal?
(JOHN 17:21) (1 TIMOTHY 1:15) (REVELATION 19:7)

For what purpose does the author say you were created?
(EPHESIANS 1:4-12) (EPHESIANS 2:10) (1 JOHN 1:3-4)

Who are some of the people in the Bible that were known as friends of God?
(EXODUS 33:11) (JAMES 2:23)

What does Jesus entrust His friends with?
(JOHN 14:12) (JOHN 20:21) (ACTS 10:42-43)

FRIENDS OF THE KING

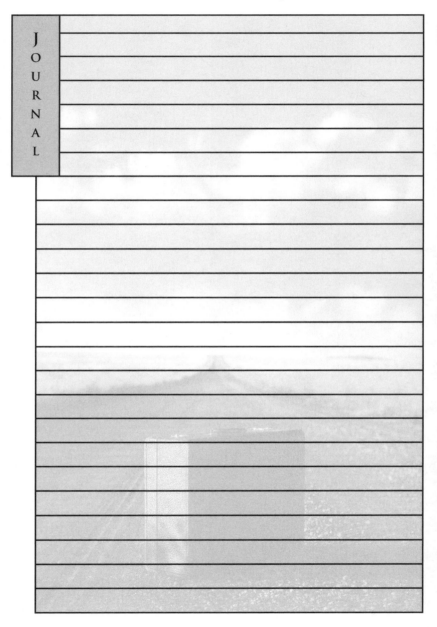

JOURNAL

CHAPTER 11

Chosen

WHY DOES GOD REVEAL HIMSELF TO PEOPLE?

God is always fulfilling His purposes in this world. At the heart of the matter is the simple truth that God wants to be known. Since He yearns for companionship, He chooses men and women to reveal Himself to them. Men and women are His most important creation and truly His finest creative workmanship. Above all things, we are created for His pleasure. At times men and women are invited to become coworkers with Him. Often we are given opportunities to express our own creative abilities which reflect His creative nature in us. In this environment there is an ongoing realization that every new invention and every discovery comes from God who is the source of all creativity and all creation. All creation is designed to draw us to God.

As children of God, we carry the genetic spiritual blueprint of our heavenly Father. Our Father in Heaven is relational at the core of His being. His relational orientation compels Him to progressively reveal Himself in us and through us. The result of this revelation consequently stimulates a vital developing connection with man. This connection is at the center of our reason for being. The entire process of revelation encourages interaction and communication which normally leads to a deeper and richer relationship. If we have learned anything as we progress on this spiritual journey, it is that the King and His Kingdom are all about relationship

(**REFERENCES:** JOHN 1:1-18, JOHN 20:30-31, EPHESIANS 1:3-14, 1 JOHN 1:1-5)

Whose idea was it that you should be a friend of God? (JOHN 15:16)

What things does God look for when He chooses His friends? (PSALM 4:3) (ISAIAH 57:15) (MICAH 6:8) (JOHN 1:47)

How important is the spiritual ability to "hear" with spiritual ears? (MATTHEW 11:15) (MATTHEW 13:43) (MARK 4:22-25)

How does hearing precede healing according to the prophet Isaiah? (ISAIAH 6:9-10)

What is another primary trait of "godly" men or women in the Bible?
(MARK 8:18) (LUKE 1:76-80) (JOHN 1:51)

How does faith work as it relates to spiritually seeing into the realm of the unseen world?
(ROMANS 4:13-24)

Explain what it means to have "a heart for God."
(MATTHEW 5:8)

What is the biggest problem when it comes to the heart condition of the masses?
(JEREMIAH 17:9) (MARK 7:6)

What great promise does God make those whose hearts are far away from Him?
(JEREMIAH 32:40) (EZEKIEL 36:26)

Jesus spoke about the root cause of defilement or being unclean. Describe it.
(MATTHEW 12:34) (MARK 7:15)

Did Jesus warn His closest followers about the cause of spiritual blindness?
(MARK 8:17-18) (MARK 16:14)

According to the author, what is the greatest asset a man or woman of God can possess?
(LUKE 1:38) (LUKE 8:15) (1 TIMOTHY 1:5)

When God has truly touched a man, what comes out of the man?
(Luke 1:46-55) (John 4:27-30)

CHOSEN

JOURNAL

CHAPTER 12

Mystical Union

WHY WOULD GOD WANT TO BE UNITED WITH MAN?

In union there exists the possibility of reproduction. God as Creator continues to create when He is united with His new creation, man. God makes more of what He is when He is one with man. The coming together of God and man allows Him to reproduce Himself over and over in some sense through the man who is one with Him. In a limited measure, incarnation occurs repeatedly allowing God to live His life out through His people. The Bible calls this "Christ in you, the hope of glory" (Colossians 2:27).

The result of this shared life is fruitfulness and reproduction. God's qualities and His attributes are multiplied in His creation through His union with those who are one with Him. He is thus able to appropriate the benefits of salvation that He brought about in Christ Jesus. Through a Body of Christ with many members who are united to Him, God reaches to the ends of the earth with the message of His redeeming love.

(REFERENCES: GENESIS 1:26-28, JOHN 15:16, EPHESIANS 1:3-14, REVELATION 21:1-27)

The reality of the Kingdom of God is manifested in three things. Describe them.
(ROMANS 14:7)

Explain the context in which the Kingdom of God is revealed.
(PHILIPPIANS 2:7-16)

How is the Kingdom both visible and invisible?
(JOHN 4:23-24) (JOHN 14:9) (ROMANS 1:19-20)

How is a spiritual man born?
(ROMANS 10:10) (1 PETER 1:23)

Describe the new creation man.
(JOHN 17:6) (2 CORINTHIANS 5:17) (COLOSSIANS 3:1-17)

The spiritual man is different from the natural man in what ways?
(JOHN 6:63) (1 CORINTHIANS 15:40-49)

What can the union of God and man be compared to in the natural realm?
(MARK 10:6-9) (EPHESIANS 5:25-32)

What does God want to produce as a result of His union with man?
(GENESIS 1:28) (JOHN 15:4-8)

How would you describe the final result of God's union with man?
(JOHN 15:16) (1 CORINTHIANS 12:12) (COLOSSIANS 1:26-30)

In what ways does God reproduce Himself in mankind?
(JOHN 3:6) (ROMANS 8:14-19) (1 PETER 1:23)

When God expresses Himself, it often takes a shape that looks like a man.

Where then do we see Jesus living His life out in our days?
(MATTHEW 25:34-45) (COLOSSIANS 1:27) (1 PETER 1:14)

Mystical Union

A Traveler's Guide to the Spirit Realm

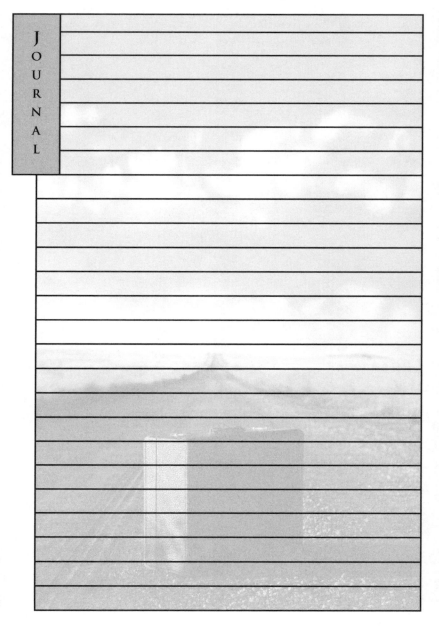

J
O
U
R
N
A
L

The Man Is the Message

HOW CAN A PERSON SPEAK FOR GOD?

While it seems almost incomprehensible to the human mind that God would speak through men and women, nevertheless God has chosen to reveal Himself in this most interesting manner. As a man or woman comes to know God, the life of God on the inside begins to shape the character of that man or woman. Over a period of time, the knowledge of God produces a new lifestyle, new attitudes, and godly thought processes that reflect the God who lives in man.

The indwelling Christ is the biblical concept for God's life in a man or woman. The indwelling Christ seeks to be made known as the revealer of God. Essentially, the life of God is so distinct from the life of the flesh or earthly nature of man, that the distinction is usually quite visible when communicated in word and deed. A person who is full of God or full of His Spirit speaks for God as God takes over on the inside of the person. The outward man simply functions as a tent or house to cover the inward speaking and self-revealing God. The person becomes an ambassador for the Lord while carrying the very life of God in his natural human body.

This revelation of God's life in a person can be both seen and heard. The redeemed person is the vessel, but the life and the voice come from God. This is a great and wonderful mystery that progressively unfolds as the spiritual seeker moves fully into the Kingdom. This mystery is foundational to the truth that God wants to be known by man.

(**REFERENCES:** ACTS 1:8, EPHESIANS 6:19-20, COLOSSIANS 1:24-29, REVELATION 1:9-18)

The author says that a logical result of the union of God is that a man becomes the message of God to the world. What does this mean to you?

How is Jesus the message of God to the world? (JOHN 1:14-17) (EPHESIANS 1:9-10)

What does the writer of the second book of Corinthians mean by "living letters"? (2 CORINTHIANS 3:2-8)

How does a man become the revelation of God in his generation? (MATTHEW 4:19) (2 CORINTHIANS 4:1-15)

Why does God use men and women to tell His story?
(ROMANS 10:12-15) (REVELATION 12:11)

What two things does the preacher speak with?
(LUKE 6:45) (1 CORINTHIANS 16:13) (JAMES 2:14-18)

When the words a man speaks are contrary to the life
he lives, how do people respond?
(MATTHEW 7:3-5)

How should we then live?
(JOHN 13:12-17) (1 PETER 1:13-22) (2 CORINTHIANS 5:11-20)

Why does the Bible say "we have this treasure in earthen vessels"?
(2 CORINTHIANS 4:7-11)

Do you hear God speaking to your inner man when you look at people with various needs, attitudes, abilities, and giftings?
(REVELATION 1:15) (REVELATION 14:2)

Why would God make us the way we are in order to reveal Himself through us?
(PSALM 139:13-16) (LUKE 7:35)

What do you think that God is saying to the world through you?
(REVELATION 22:17)

JOURNAL

THE MAN IS THE MESSAGE

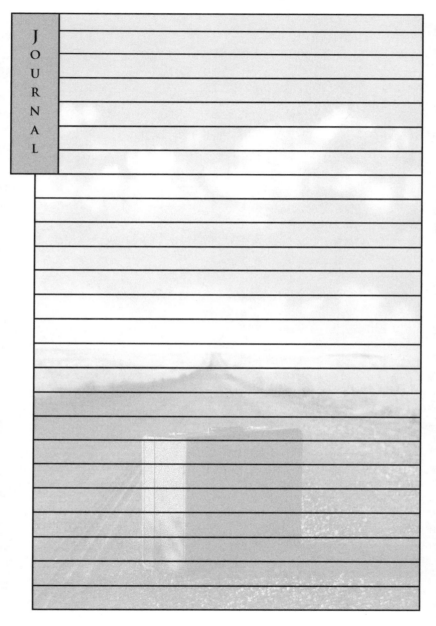

JOURNAL

CHAPTER 14

Tellers of the Truth

WHY DO THE PEOPLE WHO MEET GOD ALWAYS WANT TO TALK ABOUT HIM?

Perhaps we can best describe Heavenly encounters as those experiences that are truly worth talking about. It is the common reaction to the uncommon encounter with God that makes us speak. Every encounter with the invisible One validates the hope and inner conviction that there must be more to life than initially meets the eye. Personal experiences with God are often transforming events for the individual. It is easy to see how the people who have been changed by their divine encounters would want others to know the truth too.

In the economy of God, revelation almost always produces a reaction in a cause and effect manner. One word from God can change a man who can change a nation. Like a rock that is thrown into the middle of a pond, there is a predictable ripple effect that moves across the entire pond. Communication is the normal result of revelation. It is one of the amazing realities inherent to the Kingdom of God.

(REFERENCES: ISAIAH 6:1-8, JEREMIAH 20:9, LUKE 1:67-79, JOHN 20:21, ROMANS 10:8-15)

The writer says that God wants something. Explain what God really wants.
(EXODUS 6:2-8) (PSALM 9:16) (PSALM 98:1-2) (EZEKIEL 39:7) (JOHN 1:6-8)

Describe what usually happens to a person who has had an encounter with the Lord.
(EXODUS 3:3-12) (ISAIAH 6:1-6) (1 PETER 2:9-10)

Why do people tend to tell about their encounters with the living God?
(PSALM 22:22) (PSALM 66:16) (PSALM 96:3) (PSALM 145:6) (MATTHEW 28:7)

What does the author say about the root revelation of the Kingdom of God?
(DEUTERONOMY 29:29)

How does God preach?
(HEBREWS 12:1) (ACTS 1:8) (REVELATION 19:6)

In what ways does nature declare the greatness of God?
(PSALM 19) (PSALM 29:3-9) (PSALM 145:10-13)

How would you describe the connection between revelation and communication?
(ACTS 26:1-29)

Do you believe that the truth will always eventually be told?

The author uses the phrase "show-and-tell." How would this concept apply to your life?

TELLERS OF THE TRUTH

JOURNAL

CHAPTER 15

Granted

WHAT GREAT PRIVILEGE HAS BEEN GIVEN TO MEN AND WOMEN?

Life itself is the privilege and gift of God to men. Life flows out of relationship which is inherently part of the privilege given to men and women by God. Jesus gives Himself to us and therefore gives us life. God gives Himself and offers a life-producing relationship. In successive acts of revelation, God reveals Himself that we might know Him. It is in knowing Him that the scripture declares that we have life. Without a revelation of God in His self-giving excellence, humankind is for all intents and purposes, lifeless.

When God extends an invitation for us to meet Him, we join the ranks of the privileged that can then choose life over death. This is the greatest gift that God could ever give to us as human beings. He gives Himself that we might know Him, gain Him, and be found in Him. This is life in its fullest sense. The free gift of God is abundant and everlasting life to all who seek Him. His promise to those who seek Him is that they will find Him when they search for Him with all their heart.... It is the adventure of a lifetime, and the one journey that is surely worth taking.

(REFERENCES: JOHN 5:20-24, PHILIPPIANS 3:7-16, 2 PETER 1:2-4, 1 JOHN 3:1-10)

Why do some people go through life without ever seeing the hidden Kingdom of God?
(LUKE 8:9-10)

How does the life of Jesus show us the secrets of the Kingdom of God?
(1 JOHN 1:1-5)

Who understands the mysteries of the Kingdom of God?
(DANIEL 2:28-30) (MATTHEW 13:10-12) (1 CORINTHIANS 4:1)

What does the phrase mean, "Unto you it has been granted to know"?
(JOHN 3:27) (JOHN 6:65)

Where are all the treasures of wisdom and knowledge hidden?
(ISAIAH 45:3) (COLOSSIANS 2:3)

What is the greatest gift that God can give?
(JOHN 3:16) (1 JOHN 4:9-10)

In what ways is Jesus the indescribable great gift of God to man?
(JOHN 4:10-14) (ROMANS 6:23) (2 CORINTHIANS 9:15) (EPHESIANS 1:18-23)

How is Jesus life?
(JOHN 1:4) (JOHN 7:37-38) (JOHN 11:25) (JOHN 17:3)

What kind of things do Kingdom priests do?
(ROMANS 12:1) (HEBREWS 13:15) (REVELATION 1:6)

Why do we need authority to rule over every lower thing that lives in the present realm?
(GALATIANS 5:16-24) (2 PETER 1:2-11)

Is there anything that can conquer King Jesus?
(1 CORINTHIANS 15:26) (1 CORINTHIANS 15:57) (REVELATION 19:15)

Where is every other mystery of God revealed?
(COLOSSIANS 2:3)

Why would the author describe this narrative of the Kingdom as a journey?
(JOHN 12:35-36) (ROMANS 6:4) (GALATIANS 5:16) (EPHESIANS 5:1) (COLOSSIANS 1:10)

Where would you say you are on the journey with the King?
(1 TIMOTHY 4:16) (2 PETER 3:14-15)

Where would the King say you are on the journey with Him?

A Traveler's Guide to the Spirit Realm

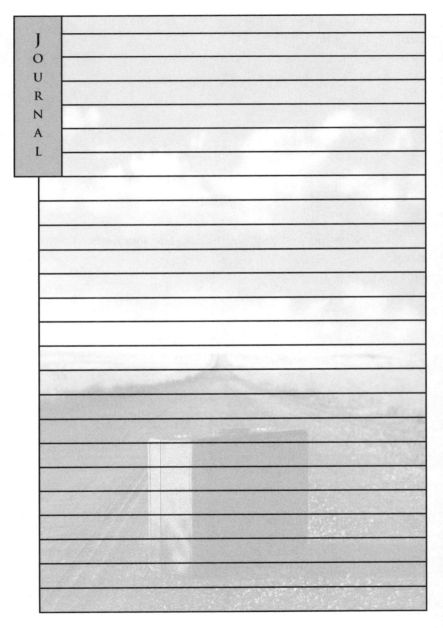

JOURNAL

GRANTED

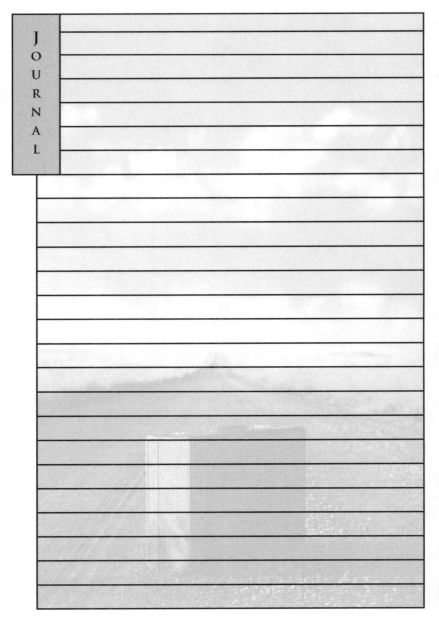

JOURNAL

About the Author

Mark Van Deman is a preacher and a teacher. He and his wife Susan have been seeking the Lord for a long time. The Lord called them into ministry when they were in their twenties. They felt especially that the Lord wanted them to take a stand for the Word of God, for righteousness, and for family values. They believed God for a family that would honor Him in the midst of a generation that knew little of the blessing of children and the sacredness of marriage. Today they have nine sons, four daughter-in-laws, several grandchildren, and can believe for much more. Their entire family is a sign of the faithfulness and goodness of God.

The Lord has allowed Mark to preach all over the world. People in Africa, India, South America, and in the United States like to hear about his family and his stories about Jesus and the kingdom of God. Mark's simple goal in life is to please the Lord. Above all things, he takes the call of God and his family commitments seriously.

A Traveler's Guide to the Spirit Realm, (Unlocking the Mysteries to the Kingdom) came about as a result of three specific Divine encounters Mark had many years ago while he was in seminary working on his Masters degree. He finally wrote it out so that he could tell the truth to more folks. The Lord has blessed Mark with some insight and revelation from the Bible which has become the foundation for his ministry to the nations, to his community, to his family, and friends. He hopes that the things revealed will help people to know Jesus and live forever.

Mark and Susan reside in Whiteland, Indiana where they can see the ends of the world.

It is their desire to communicate the Word of God with clarity and power. Their plan is to love Jesus and love people and involve a lot of other people in the plan. If the Lord lets them live a while longer, they will probably do a lot of other fun things too.

Author Contact Information

Mark Van Deman
PO Box 205
Whiteland, IN 46184
Website: markvandeman.com

Additional copies of this book and other book titles from DESTINY IMAGE are available at your local bookstore.

Call toll-free: 1-800-722-6774.

Send a request for a catalog to:

Destiny Image® Publishers, Inc.
P.O. Box 310
Shippensburg, PA 17257-0310

"Speaking to the Purposes of God for this Generation and for the Generations to Come."

For a complete list of our titles, visit us at www.destinyimage.com.